Critical Acclaim for *Sand in My Bra*

"These snappy travel stories bursting with candor and crackling humor are sure to leave readers feeling that to not have an adventure to remember is a great loss indeed. *Sand in My Bra* will light a fire under the behinds of, as the dedication states, 'all the women who sit at home or behind their desks bitching that they never get to go anywhere.'"

—*Publishers Weekly*

"A collection of ridiculous and sublime travel experiences."

—*San Francisco Chronicle* Best-Seller List

"Reading about someone else's troubles can be devastatingly funny. And so we have in this volume exotic settings, language-based miscommunication, and not-always-pleasant surprises as things do not go as planned. Despite it all, our band of female travel writers laughs heartily, with pen, paper and laptop at the quick."

—*Chicago Tribune*

"The writers in *Sand in My Bra* revel in the absurdities of life away from home. F★★k epiphanies; these are the sort of yarns that leave me itching to hit the road."

—*BUST*

"Hip chicks with a flair for storytelling share travel tales in *Sand in My Bra*. From reveling in the "freedom to be fat" in Tahiti to cycling topless at the Burning Man festival in Nevada, the stories celebrate the unexpected joys of travel from a feminine perspective."

—*Orlando Sentinel*

"Good-natured women find the funny side of mishaps in places as far flung as the red-light district in Bangkok and a 50-pound sack race in small-town Nevada. There are plenty of laughs and—a side benefit—some handy warnings on what not to do when traveling."

—*Portsmith Herald*

"A delightfully entertaining look at atypical travel experiences."

—*South Coast Beacon*

"*Sand in My Bra* supplies laughs as well as a quick fix for the homebound yearning for a quick walk on the wild side."

—*St. Petersburg Times*

Travelers' Tales Books

Country and Regional Guides

America, Australia, Brazil, Central America, Cuba, France, Greece, India, Ireland, Italy, Japan, Mexico, Nepal, Spain, Thailand, Tibet, Turkey; American Southwest, Grand Canyon, Hawai'i, Hong Kong, Paris, Provence, San Francisco, Tuscany

Women's Travel

Her Fork in the Road, A Woman's Path, A Woman's Passion for Travel, A Woman's World, Women in the Wild, A Mother's World, Safety and Security for Women Who Travel, Gutsy Women, Gutsy Mamas

Body & Soul

The Spiritual Gifts of Travel, The Road Within, Love & Romance, Food, The Fearless Diner, The Adventure of Food, The Ultimate Journey, Pilgrimage

Special Interest

Sand in My Bra and Other Misadventures, Not So Funny When It Happened, The Gift of Rivers, Shitting Pretty, Testosterone Planet, Danger!, The Fearless Shopper, The Penny Pincher's Passport to Luxury Travel, The Gift of Birds, Family Travel, A Dog's World, There's No Toilet Paper on the Road Less Traveled, The Gift of Travel, 365 Travel, Adventures in Wine

Footsteps

Kite Strings of the Southern Cross, The Sword of Heaven, Storm, Take Me With You, Last Trout in Venice, The Way of the Wanderer, One Year Off, The Fire Never Dies

Classics

The Royal Road to Romance, Unbeaten Tracks in Japan, The Rivers Ran East, Coast to Coast, Trader Horn

TRAVELERS' TALES

sand in *My Bra*

and Other Misadventures

funny women write from the road

Travelers' Tales

sand in *My Bra*

and Other Misadventures

funny women write from the road

Edited by
JENNIFER L. LEO

Series Editors
James O'Reilly and Larry Habegger

Travelers' Tales
San Francisco

Art Direction: Michele Wetherbee
Interior design: Kathryn Heflin and Susan Bailey
Cover photograph: © 2001, Hovering. "Omar Kabish the Fish" by Kathleen and Frank Walker crosses the playa at Burning Man 2001.
Page layout: Cynthia Lamb using the fonts Bembo and Journal

Distributed by: Publishers Group West, 1700 Fourth Street, Berkeley, California 94710.

Library of Congress Cataloging-in-Publication Data

Sand in my bra and other misadventures: funny women write from the road / edited by Jennifer L. Leo — 1st ed.
p. cm.
ISBN 1-885211-92-9 (pbk.)
1. Women travelers. 2. Voyages and travels. I. Leo, Jennifer.

G465 . S248 2003
910.4'082—dc21

2003005512

First Edition
Printed in the United States
10 9 8 7 6

For all the women who sit at home or behind their desks bitching that they never get to go anywhere.

Table of Contents

Introduction

JESSICA MAXWELL

We were sitting under a beat-up blue gazebo waiting for a panga boat to take us into the heart of Trinidad's Caroni Swamp. Tony, our driver, suddenly scowled at the hip young man smooching with his girlfriend on the bench across from ours.

"I can't stand to see a man wearing a earring!" he muttered.

Chris, our photographer, was busy eyeing the Caribbean wasps swarming around a nest above our heads. He thought Tony had said he couldn't stand seeing a man eating a herring.

"Yeah," Chris replied. "They make me sick, too."

"Dey look so feminine!" Tony spat.

Chris glanced at him sideways.

"I never thought they looked feminine," he answered. "I just think they smell funny."

Tony's head snapped in Chris's direction.

"You theenk dey *smell* funny?"

"Yeah, especially if you eat them."

"You *EAT* dem?"

"No! I told you, they make me sick!"

Fortunately, the panga arrived in time to avoid an international incident, but I have long considered this conversation to be the perfect example of travel hilarity. It has it all: an exotic setting, great characters, communication snafus, and a who-the-heck-knows-what-will-happen-next spirit of cultural collision. If you think about it, how could travel be anything *but* funny? Especially for women.

Only while traveling could a woman find herself being followed around by a Frenchman asking her if she "would like a snake," when he only wants to buy her a sandwich. Where else could she consult a dictionary for the Lebanese words for "pop" and "corn," then try asking for some popcorn at a local supermarket only to learn from the kindly Englishman standing behind her that she has just requested a package of elephant farts? Only in Mexico could she look at a flower seller's pretty little daughter and announce to the child that her mother has a lovely garlic. And only in Spain could she order a tortilla and end up with an omelet as if she learned nothing on her trip to Mexico at all.

As a life-long travel writer, I've learned to expect this sort of thing.

And worse.

I once took a girlfriend with me on a nature assignment in Provence. I thought it would cheer her up after a bad break-up with her boyfriend. We were supposed to report back on the tens of thousands of waterfowl that stop in the Camargue wetlands each November during their winter migration south, and we arrived in Paris as chirpy as a couple of baby chicks ourselves. But we couldn't find our hotel—the instructions had failed to mention that one—and only one—little tiny two-foot invisible street led to the hotel's front door, so we circled the place like vultures for three full hours before we figured it out.

The next morning, happy again, we began our drive to Provence, only to come to a dead stop half an hour later. The French truck drivers were on strike and a fleet of them had parked in the middle of the autoroute. It took another hour to maneuver *off* the freeway, then another day and a half on traffic-jammed back roads to reach Arles. We arrived at midnight two days late, and when with great emotion in not-so-bad French I tried to explain things to the hotel manager, she looked at us with ice pick eyes and said:

"Eef you panic, I ham going straight to bed!"

After she brutally berated my friend for bring bakery croissants to our room the next morning we fled to the Camargue, only to find that it was flooded and the birds were all *dispersee*. We counted exactly two ducks, and that included the dead one a chef insisted on cooking for lunch for us when he heard of our plight.

Back in Paris the night before our departure I tried to save the day by taking my friend to a fancy restaurant…so fancy even I, who have lived in France, couldn't understand anything on the menu. At that point my poor friend burst into tears.

"I *hate* this country!" she wailed. "They take all your money, they treat you like dirt and you can't even read the f——ing menu!"

And that's when Mario showed up. A pony-tailed Italian designer in lemon-yellow pants and a lime-green blazer with a rainbow-colored parrot pin on one lapel, he was in Paris to teach at the Sorbonne for the winter. Without asking, he took a seat at our table and began patting my friend's arm.

"You are-a rright-a!" he said. "Thee French, they are-a crazy. They-a always got-a problem. Always something-a wrong-a. They don't-a know-a how to-a live-a. You come to-a Italy! We take-a better care of-a you!"

My friend started laughing. Then she got hysterical. Which made all of us get hysterical with her. Pretty soon everyone in the restaurant was sharing in this marvelous emotional catharsis, including the restaurant owner who insisted on ordering for us then refused to let us pay him a franc for what was the singularly best meal either of us had ever had. And my friend flew home healed.

This simply couldn't have happened in Chicago. Or Seattle. Or Atlanta. Or New York. Well, maybe in New York, but it wouldn't have been half as funny. To this day, that's how we remember that trip: hilarious! Banished from memory are the anguish, frustration, tears, fear and loathing, even that horror story of a hotel manager. All we remember is the ridiculousness of it all, and it's an experience that bonds us to this day.

What does this teach those of us who love to travel the globe? Let your smile be your umbrella!...and trash can and shield. Foreign travel simply does not always go smoothly. It *can't*. There are too many moving parts. So rather than think of it as a booby-trap, think of it as your big chance to play Lucille-Ball-Goes-on-Vacation. If you can make peace with the concept of travel as a comedy-waiting-to-happen, then almost nothing can rob you of the deeper thrill of it. The delight of eating your first Provençal truffle, the joy of setting foot finally on your Irish grandmother's homeland, the rush of breathing in the cold wind of the Himalayas, the delirium of making love to your good familiar husband while the sweet smoke of temple incense twists into your window from the Kyoto monastery across the street.

This is the heart of travel. This is why we do it. This is why we are so willing to strap our fragile bodies into metal capsules and fly thousands of miles with hundreds of strangers endlessly exhaling new viruses into our airspace, drink water from dubious sources, eat food virulent with unknown flora and fauna, put up with impossible travel companions, lost luggage, and the legions of mule-like bureaucrats who manage to win positions of petty power in every city and village on earth. We do it because we love this beautiful dangerous planet and we want to know it personally and, on balance, the pluses far outweigh the minuses, right?

That's what the women in *Sand in My Bra* know, too. When Joann Hornak saves herself from a herd of wild elephants in "Fifteen Minutes Can Last Forever," she sees the folly in taking the advice of a would-be Tarzan. When Christine Michaud in "Chador Etiquette" tries to dress like the locals in Kuwait in a chador many sizes too small, she realizes that "going unnoticed" is sometimes impossible. When Michelle Peterson in "Hat Head" has a bad hair day in Hong Kong, she discovers salvation, and a nice human connection, via a sampan pilot's hat. And when Christine Nielsen gets sand in her bra (and everywhere else) at the wacky Burning Man festival in the Nevada desert, she knows it's just all part of the fun.

So, think of travel as a sort of fast-forward Zen meditation, an act of supreme balance while off-balance, a living devotion to the notion of Love Thy Neighbor even if he happens to be a very drunk German singing Oktoberfest songs under your window at three A.M. And if you can manage to see the humor in *that*, then the cosmic joke is forever on this goofy world of ours, not you.

Originally, Jessica Maxwell wanted to be a serious environmental reporter—until her first assignment, on the Los Angeles sewer system, went south when she learned that the treatment plant's supervisor was named Arthur F. Suher. She turned to serious travel writing. "That was like trying to organize raw egg whites," she says. "Everything gets scrambled and pretty soon all you want is breakfast." This made her turn to serious food writing, which soured when a customs officer refused to let her take Oregon truffles into France, despite—or perhaps because of—her claims that truffles are "scientifically neither animal nor plant and are, in fact, closer to humans, DNA-wise." Next she took up serious golf writing, only to learn that golf is "just too weird," but mean editors made her write a whole book on the subject anyway. She is the author of books on golf, fly fishing, and international travel, and continues to write for magazines specializing in what she calls the "literary culinary conservation sporting travel narrative," which is about to take another artistic turn with her fourth book, a "serious spiritual adventure about karmic love, Buddhist golf, jokester ghosts and an unexpected lunch with Deepak Chopra." Maxwell lives with her extremely tolerant trial attorney husband and part-bobcat kitty in Eugene, Oregon.

KARLA ZIMMERMAN

Mom's Travel Advisories

Sometimes problems begin before *departure.*

GUERRILLAS. DRUG LORDS. LANDMINES. LIMB LOSS. Organ Malfunction.

According to my mother, these are just a few of the terrors that await me when I arrive in South America. It doesn't matter that for the past ten years I've traveled to and returned safely from dubious destinations such as Guatemala, India, Russia, and Corsica. To Mom, each new journey is fresh ground for death. Which is why she demands that I visit her before each trip.

"What if you get killed while you're away?" she reasons. "Your dad and I want to see you before that happens."

When I arrive home, Mom begins reviewing her extensive checklist of safety precautions:

"Make sure you put my name and address in your passport," she instructs. "That way, when you get knocked upside the head by a dope fiend or drop dead from an appendicitis attack, the Chileans who find you will know where to send the body."

She makes a mark on her note pad. "Now, are you taking the proper medicines to stay healthy while you're away?"

"I got all of my immunizations, and I'll carry a small first aid kit for emergencies," I hold up my hand and testify.

"That's sweet," Mom smiles. "But I'm talking about the hard stuff—to ease the pain when you get shot by Peruvian guerrillas or lose a limb to a Colombian landmine."

After loading my pack with an Elvis-worthy sedative supply, Mom checks her list again, then blanches.

"Hey, you won't wear shorts while you're there, will you?

"N…"

"Good," she snaps, before my "o" hits the air. "Because some drugged-up Argentinean sex maniac will find it suggestive if you go around looking like Charo."

"Charo's from Spain," I start to explain, but Mom holds up her hand.

"How about a hat? Are you going to wear a hat while you're in Bolivia? You should disguise your looks. Wear shades. Maybe I should buy you a pair of fake buck teeth."

"I'm taking a baseball cap and these sunglasses," I say, and put them on.

"On second thought," she frowns, "forget the shades. They look kind of sexy."

To help assuage Mom's fears, I give her a detailed itinerary with flight numbers and hotel names. I produce newspaper articles with pretty pictures of my destinations, and reassuring Centers for Disease Control health briefs that I find on-line. I invite over friends who have traveled to South America, so they can provide encouraging stories on how clean and kind the people are. I promise to call home once a week.

"Mom?" I ask gently, after my friends have left, "are you still worried?"

"I'm not worried," she says, looking up from my pack, where she is slipping in a socket wrench and an extra pair of boots. "My friends—particularly Maryann, my hairdresser, who is a big wimp—they're the ones who fear for your safety. I always have to tell them, 'My girl can take care of herself.'"

But the more she reassures me—and she does so thirteen times over the course of two days—the more I know she is worried.

With this in mind, I think I'll refrain from telling her my newest discovery: that I'm arriving at my first destination—Santiago, Chile—during Terrorist Week. The State Department warning is not severe, a small sidebar about the country's national holiday and the demonstrations and government protests that can accompany it.

But thanks to Mom, a voice inside my head shouts, "Wear dark colors, so you won't stand out to kidnappers who will remove your appendix using an unsterilized hacksaw. Organ trafficking is big in Chile."

But it's also thanks to Mom that I can push that aside, secure in the knowledge that 4,000 miles away, someone is looking out for me—and available to receive my remains, should there be any.

Karla Zimmerman lives in Chicago. She recently returned from traveling in South America, where—in her attempt to speak Spanish—she told everyone she was an "escritoria," *which she thought was the word for "writer." Alas, now that she's home, she's found out that it means "desk."*

GERMAINE W. SHAMES

Mexican Mating Calls

The author raises the eternal question: Is love amphibious?

ONCE I HAD A LOVER—LET'S CALL HIM JUAN—WHOSE English was, at best, rudimentary. But Juan spoke the universal language like a master. On his silvery tongue, even the most garbled expressions took my breath away.

Juan and I met in Mexico, his country of birth, my temporary residence. Land of the *piropo* (verbal tributes to feminine charms), of long songs and laments, Mexico was the perfect setting for a storybook romance, and Juan, as I said, was well-suited to the role of Don Juan.

"My love, my heart, my life," he'd croon, looking deep into my eyes with a fiery gaze that made my heart smolder, "I love you with every breath I take, I can't live without you. You are the queen of my existence, and I your slave."

Whether or not I believed Juan, I can't really say. So dazzled was I by his declarations of love, so mesmerized by the burning look that accompanied them, discernment failed me. Juan made me feel desired, cherished, worshipped. His words entered my bloodstream like an elixir and made my heart *cha-cha-cha*. In love with Juan's verbiage, I let it work its magic and asked no questions.

Life with Juan was all-day siestas and all-night fiestas, serenades at my balcony, roses at my doorstep, and Juan pinned to my ear, cooing his inimitable Mexican mating calls.

"My nightingale, my heaven, my saint," he'd tell me, letting the words trickle down my earlobe like warm honey. "I love you with every beat of my heart. You're part of my very being, as essential as the air I breathe. If you left me, I swear I would die."

Leave Juan? I supposed I might one day, but I was in no hurry. Life as Juan's *novia* (sweetheart) was sweet indeed. As long as the nectar in Juan's tongue continued to flow, I saw no reason for our idyll to end. Latin courtships might last months, years, long enough for me to soak up volumes of Juan's odes and oaths.

"My light, my soul, my treasure," he'd whisper endlessly, growing bolder, drawing me closer, so close I could see the facets in his eyes glow like hot coals. "I love you more than I love myself, more that your own mother loves you, more than—may the Virgin forgive me!—more than God Himself could ever love you. I swear I would die for you."

Fortunately for most Juans, few loves are ever actually put to the test. No doubt, my Juan banked on not having to make good on his claims. He was only telling me what I wanted to hear, after all: words of love.

But, as fate would have it, circumstances intervened—drastic circumstances—that thrust my very life into his hands.

One weekend Juan took me to a small seaside resort outside Playa Blanca where we intended to spend a few quiet days romancing to the rhythm of the waves. The setting—white-hot sands, placid sea, a caressing breeze—had all the promise of a sultry summer daydream. Shortly after our arrival, however, a nasty storm blew in, and the tide rose like a waterfall in reverse.

For two days Juan and I kept to our sweltering hotel room, glued together by our own perspiration. Whatever the mosquitoes spared of me, Juan nibbled at unceasingly, until every pore of my body stung. By day three—the last of our little holiday—raw, dehydrated, half-incinerated, I decided to have a swim come what may.

Out I ran to the beach with Juan calling after me, "My love, the sea she's mean. Don't go!"

He was right. I was no match for the waves, and they had their way with me. Tossed about like a dummy, suctioned down into the drink again and again, I quickly felt my fight give out. I was drowning.

"Help me, Juan!" I screamed. My mouth filled with brine each time I opened it. "Help me! Help! Help…!"

"Sweem, *mamacita*, sweem!" Juan cried back.

"Help!" I cried desperately, a dozen times, a hundred, though Juan had no doubt heard me the first time.

"Sweem, *por Dios* (for God's sake)! Sweem!" he repeated, matching me yelp for yelp.

The poor man was beside himself, clearly. He ran up and down the beach, weeping, wailing; he tore his hair, waved his arms, fell to his knees…and never so much as wet the tips of his toes.

When a wayward wave finally heaved me onto the beach where he waited dry and safe, I couldn't help but feel sorry for him. Not meaning to, I had exposed him; his words had been so much flotsam.

But Juan showed no signs of embarrassment. To the contrary, his face lit up and he shed tears of joy.

"My goddess, my angel, my adoration..." he cooed, riveting me once more with his searing gaze as he led me away.

Germaine W. Shames is author of the critically acclaimed travelers' novel, Between Two Deserts. *Shames has written from six continents—soon to add the seventh—on topics ranging from the Middle East crisis to the plight of street children. Her essays and short fiction have been widely anthologized; her articles appear in such periodicals as* National Geographic Traveler, Hemispheres, *and* Success. *She was last spotted piloting a narrow boat up the Grand Union Canal, accompanied by an Anglicized gorilla.*

COLETTE O'CONNOR

* * *

Internal Affairs

A woman explores the Kingdom of Euphemism.

"MADAME!" THE RECEPTIONIST BECKONS. GINGERLY, my alarming symptom and I sit where she motions, here in the foyer of a Paris gynecologist's office. The chairs are Louis something and gold frou-frou gilds the walls in that fancy French style so swell in a château but frankly not the sort of comfort I need now that the doctor refuses to see me. Not until I fill out the fat clipboard of forms on my lap, that is, and bypass the problem that has me stalled and gnawing my pencil at Question 2: "What brings you to the doctor today?" Through the smoked glass door to the examination room I see the shadow of him hiding in back; he is perched on a stool, twiddling his instruments, waiting. His concern hangs on him like his white coat two sizes too big—just about the size mine should be for I have recently discovered a secret so hush-hush here in France that any American worth her women's rights would marvel at the good fortune: here, there is no "down there."

That's right. For millions of Frenchwomen, when it comes

to the subject of their bodies, here, there are no ovaries to speak of, no fallopian tubes to point out, no uterus to note, or vagina. Nor are there breasts or PMS. If that sounds bad, what's worse is the alarming symptom I woke up with today is located in a place on my body which in France is not on the map, territory as yet uncharted, for no words exist to describe it.

My French friend, Eve-Marie, first shared the shocking fact of her country's lack of even a single serviceable cervix the June day we strolled the Champs Elysées, shopping.

"I must visit the pharmacist for my little business affair," she said suddenly, stopping in to purchase some tampons. Although Eve-Marie spoke in French, the English translation that sprung into my head was as literal as I could get. "I'll get some Pamprin, too," she added, "for my difficulty of the stomach."

"You mean, menstrual cramps, *non*?" I asked. My friend stared at me with an expression as vacant as those of the stone statues in the Louvre.

"Comment?" she said, listlessly, and I translated, "Hunh?"

Once at the drugstore, Eve-Marie was more forthright. "I would like something, *s'il vous plaît*, for my abdomen itch," she commanded and the pharmacist without so much as a mouth twitch of confusion slapped onto the counter a box of Monistat 7. *"Voilà."*

Eve-Marie! I thought, flabbergasted. Abdomen itch? Why, the way she, a grown woman, verbally tip-toed around her bodily topics seemed a show of immaturity no better than if she'd confessed to her gynecologist some trouble with her "tee-tee," or suggested to her husband that he be more attentive to her "fou-fou" in bed. Embarrassing.

I confronted her later over coffee. "Eve-Marie," I said,

being firm, "surely the pharmacists of France, professionals whose life work is to dispense products for every possible intimate situation, surely they won't be shocked at the mention of, say, a yeast infection?"

"You mean abdomen itch," my friend corrected.

"I mean, when it comes to problems like your menstrual cramps..."

"*Excusez-moi*, but it's difficulty of the stomach," my friend clarified.

"...you could just explain in plain French the exact spot in your pelvic region where..."

"If it's my lingering belly thing we're talking about then don't be absurd," said Eve-Marie, by now in a bit of a snit. "The pharmacist knows enough to hand over the K-Y jelly."

Our chat left me shattered. Long ago liberated enough to call a woman's givens by their proper names, I, like many Americans, can publicly mouth without stutter the word "menstruation." I can say it, yes, "breasts," and not collapse into a heap of preteenish snickers. Yet here in France, where women's rights ostensibly are so far advanced that RU-486 has been in use for years and sunbathing topless is *de rigueur*, Eve-Marie can't bring herself to actually say "premenstrual syndrome."

"Of course, you are referring to that which arrives each month like a hair in the soup," she said when I mentioned it. Of course.

So I zap the television one day desperate to comprehend Eve-Marie's coyness and there they are: commercials for "throat supporters," which in fact are brassières; ads for a product that provides relief from the pain and bloating of your "business affair" (Pamprin); soap opera girlfriends deep in tortured conversation over the grief of a sister's "accident" (miscarriage), in tears over a mother's fatal "heart trouble" (breast cancer). I flip through Larousse's French-English dictionary frantic for an answer and there they aren't: "clitoris," "labia," "G-spot," "vagina." These and other words for women's sexual reproductive accouterments simply can't be found. Stripped. They have been stripped from the French vocabulary as smoothly as unwanted body hair after a hot wax job.

It occurs to me that the language itself might be the douche that cleanses French of all natural, healthy expressions for the nature of womanhood. After all, as one of the world's most beautiful "romance languages," it gives itself the kiss of *politesse* by practicing excellent linguistic hygiene with many things coarse in life. It pretties-up the crude, it adds glamour to the average. In France, for example, criminals are not arrested, rather, they are "invited" to jail. A "nice to meet you" upon meeting someone new in French becomes "Enchanted!" Even a backyard tool shed behind a house in Provence is known as a "château."

Obviously, in this neck of the woods a woman's parts are perfumed by expressions that leave the feminine sex to parade through life as does Catherine Denueve through those French *films noir*—as an illusion of beauty. Mystery. A symbol creature of effortless perfection. Problem is, these parts are often drenched in euphemisms so strong their very existence seems to cease and, as the pain my alarming symptom makes plain, I have a problem that must be described and "belly itch" isn't it.

"Madame!" the receptionist beckons again, anxious to retrieve her clipboard of forms. This time she slits her eyes at me for causing a scheduling logjam and keeping the doctor stool-sitting longer than he likes. *"Alors, fini?"*

Question 2 looms. Suddenly, I am seized with the peculiar perversity of a traveler an ocean from home, alone, and frankly appalled to her very pituitary by the pitiful recognition given to Frenchwomen's otherwise self-respecting sex characteristics. If Eve-Marie and her millions of French sisters can't, I decide, I will give voice to the oppressed, to the neglected. Yes, the revolution for a freely recognized PMS starts right here, right now, with me.

What am I doing in the doctor's office today? I write furiously, in capital letters to express the militancy of my ideals: "I have had a bad menstrual pain in my left ovary or maybe my fallopian tube, or else my uterus, I don't know. But one thing's for sure: the pain isn't anything that possibly can be mistaken for a soup hair."

There. I hand the receptionist my clipboard. "Well," she sniffs. "Bravo." She briskly disappears only to reappear trailing the doctor. Worry weights his head which hangs as heavy as a water balloon.

"Madame, I don't understand," he says, oozing woe. "What can we do for you today?"

Suddenly, my body cries out in pain and panic. Cramp! Suddenly, my fantasy cause doesn't seem so hot a priority. I mean, what if I, self-styled figurehead for all disenfranchised vaginas, am picked-off prematurely by a fatal faction of pelvic inflammatory disease? What if my plans for a family are assassinated here in France by an emergency hysterectomy performed right here, right now? Oh, God. My courage spontaneously aborts and I blurt in one breath: "It was right after my last little business affair when I suffered an abdomen itch followed by bad stomach difficulty. I'm scared it might be sexually transmitted heart trouble I got from my boyfriend."

"Why didn't you just say so!" rejoices the doctor, relieved. "We'll conduct an exam *tout de suite* and have you fixed up in no time. Right this way, Madame, *merci*."

And you know, he did. It was only a minor belly thing, after all, caused by my too-tight push-up throat supporter.

A native of the San Francisco Bay Area who has lived and worked around the world in such places as New York, St. Moritz, and Paris, Colette O'Connor graduated from the University of California, Berkeley with a degree in English. Her award-winning lifestyle features, travel pieces, book reviews, interviews, and essays have appeared in numerous publications, including the Los Angeles Times, The Washington Post, World Traveling, *and* America West. *She is the editor-in-chief of* Flying Adventures: The Private Aircraft Owners/Passengers Travel & Lifestyle Magazine.

*

Tourists on their first trip to Cairo inevitably get fleeced by locals, and I was no exception. Although I'm not sure how many had to bite on a hand towel to live through it.

Blame it on my taxi driver. When I shared my wish for a Halawa session—Egyptian-style depilation done with a homemade sugar-based paste—he immediately declared his wife Sammia best suited for the job.

Next thing I knew I was sitting in my underwear on my taxi driver's bed, with Saamia hard at work on my legs. The fact that we spoke no common language only began to matter when she reached for my groin. I only wanted my legs done, little did I know I would get the Bedouin treatment: removal of ALL body hair. Before I could understand what was happening to me, my underwear was off and my most intimate parts were being waxed bare.

I have a hard time imagining what could possibly be more painful than having all your pubic hair ripped off by a bully Bedouin woman. Saamia spent half an hour on my legs, and another half-hour between them. Being as stoic as I could, I held in my screams, biting hard onto the hand towel that had been thrown at me to make sure I kept quiet. So much for discovering local customs!

—Christine Michaud, "Cairo to Istanbul in a G-String"

ANNE LAMOTT

The Aunties

She never leaves home without them.

SPIRITUAL EXPERIENCES DO NOT HAPPEN FREQUENTLY at tropical vacation spots for normal people who travel well, but there is no one fitting that description around here. I wish I could get to Kathmandu for my transformations, but I can't get any farther than Mexico. I am too much of an alarmist to stay airborne much longer than that; I can only cross one or two time zones before serious decompensation sets in. I would love to go to the Caribbean someday, or India. But they're too far. In the meantime, Mexico is my training tropics.

So I was in the Mexican state of Oaxaca when I got my most recent brown-bag spiritual victory: I broke through Butt Mind in the town of Huatulco. Or at any rate, I have only had a mild case of Butt Mind since. In earlier incarnations I've spent days and entire weeks comparing my butt to everyone else's butt. Sometimes my butt was better-than, although it is definitely the butt of a mother who keeps forgetting to work out. Mostly it was worse-than. On tropical beaches it has almost always been much-worse-than. I did not expect things to be any different this time, because gravity is having its say. Also as it turned out, there were lots of teenage girls around, only a few of whom, statistically, could be expected to have droopy butts and major dimpling issues—the feta-cheese look, as one friend puts it.

I started off in heavy Butt Mind on the plane. I was with my son Sam and our best friends. There were all these teenage girls on board in tiny shorts that Sam could have borrowed. Someone less secure about her own beauty might have said, "Too many teenage girls." They were mostly youthful and bouncy and physically stunning, if you happen to find tan, lean youth attractive. But I had recently read a magazine article on Junkie Chic, society's current exhortation of drowsy, skaggy emaciation. And for some reason the article was *mostly* making me feel militantly on my own middle-aged-mother-butt side.

I was also thinking of a priest, who said that sometimes he thinks that heaven is just a new pair of glasses. I was trying to remember to wear them. I was trying to spend less time thinking about what I see and more time thinking about why I see it that way—why I continue, off and on, to see these nice sturdy high-functioning thighs with such contempt. It's so troubling to relapse in this area, especially since somewhere along the line, I have actually come to believe that a person being herself is beautiful—that contentment and acceptance and freedom are beautiful. And most important, I have discovered *I* am clinically and objectively beautiful.

I really mean this in the literal sense. I believe that if you saw me, you would say, "Wow! What a beautiful woman."

I think.

I'm almost sure.

But of course, I was thinking all these lofty things before I got to the beach.

Until recently, I was afraid to say that I am beautiful out loud for fear that people would look at each other with amusement and think to themselves, *Well, isn't that nice.* And then they would look at me with cruel scrutiny and see a thinnish woman with tired wrinkly eyes, flabby thighs, scriggly-scraggly hair, as my son once described it, and scriggly-scraggly teeth. I was afraid they would see the spidery veins on my legs and note that my bottom appears to be making a break for freedom from the confines of my swimsuit; afraid that they would notice all the parts of me that really need to have the fat vacuumed out, or at least carpet-swept. But somehow I was not afraid to say it anymore. On that plane with all these beautiful young girls walking up the aisle as if it were a runway, if someone had exhibited so much as an angstrom of doubt about my beauty, I would have said that they could come kiss my big, beautiful, dimply, droopy butt.

However, as I said, this was before I got to the beach.

After unpacking in Huatulco, I put on my best black swimsuit. It was very expensive when I got it, very alluring. The only fly in the ointment was that it no longer fit. Actually, I'm not positive it ever did, but at least I used to be able to get it on without bruising. There in my room overlooking the turquoise sea, palm tree groves, and a sky of bright light blue, as I strained to pull the suit up past my thighs, I consoled myself by remembering that there is beauty in becoming so comfortable at being a mother, and a writer; there is grace in comfortableness. And of the several things of which I'm positive, one is that if I live to be an old woman, I won't be sitting on my porch berating myself for having leapt into a swimsuit to swim in warm ocean water at every opportunity even though my thighs were dimply. Also, most helpful of all, the wife of the couple we were traveling with—our best friends—has dimply thighs and a big butt, too.

Maybe even bigger. Not that I'm comparing or anything.

Anyway. I got my suit on and waddled down to the beach.

I was not wearing a cover-up, not even a t-shirt. I had decided I was going to take my thighs and butt with me proudly wherever I went. I decided, in fact, on the way to the beach that I would treat them as if they were beloved elderly aunties, the kind who did embarrassing things at the beach, like roll their stockings into tubes around their ankles, but whom I was proud of because they were so great in every *real and important* way. So we walked along, the three of us, the aunties and I, to meet Sam and our friends in the sand. I imagined that I could feel the aunties beaming, as if they had been held captive in a dark closet too long, like Patty Hearst. Freed finally to stroll on a sandy Mexican beach: what a beautiful story.

It did not trouble me that parts of my body—the auntie parts—kept moving even after I had come to a full halt. Who cares? People just need to be soft and clean.

> We should be provided with a new body about the age of thirty or so when we have learnt to attend to it with consideration.
>
> —Freya Stark

The first girls I saw were young, nine or ten, splashing around on the rocks near the shore, pretending to be horses. One of them was catching crabs. Iguanas watched with unblinking eyes from boulders that lined the walkway, and the three girls were fearless, unself-conscious and so lovely. At nine or ten, girls still get to be fine. They've still got a couple of years before they totally forget what they do have and start obsessing about what they don't. These girls had legs like baby egrets, probably not much changed from when they were seven or eight. They were still of an age when they could play without wearing the glasses of puberty that would make them see all their flaws. Not yet measuring, not yet comparing, still able to get caught up in crabs, in iguanas and currents, lost in what is right in front of them.

I was inspired. I found Sam and our friends on the beach, and we swam all afternoon, and everything was wonderful. Then I decided to head back up to my room for a little nap before dinner. Sam stayed with our friends on the beach. The aunties and I marched along in a way both strident and shy, until we got to one of the bus stops where the vans pick up people and drive them up the steep hillside. First I was alone, and that was nice, because I got to practice acting as if it were O.K. for a person with middle-aged thighs to stand around wearing only a swimsuit like other people. I smiled, thought fondly of the aunties, imagining one as Margaret Rutherford in old age, one as Samantha's dreamy aunt Clara in *Bewitched*, who could never get her spells to work.

And then out of nowhere, like dogs from hell, four teenage girls walked toward me to wait for the van.

They weren't wearing cover-ups either, but they were lovely and firm as models—I'd say that was the main difference—*and* all in bikinis. Two of them were already perfectly tan. And suddenly my trance was broken. Suddenly it was the Emperor's New Clothes, and I stood there in all of my fatitude like the tubby little emperor with his feta-cheese gut. In my mind now I looked like someone under fluorescent lights and felt in comparison to these girls like Roy Cohn in his last days. I wanted a trap door to open at my feet. And then—this is the truth—they *looked* at me. They looked at me standing there in the bright sunlight wearing only an ill-fitting swimsuit that had been laundered more times than the funds in Oliver North's campaign chest.

But then they made a fatal mistake. They looked at each other with these amused looks—the kind I must have given flabby women in swimsuits thirty years ago. And it gave me time to have two thoughts. One was not even a thought exactly: I just looked directly back at the four of them and heard the phantom clock playing in the background of their lives, "Tick, tock...tick, tock."

The other was the realization that I knew their secret: that they didn't think *they* were O.K. They were already in the hyper self-consciousness of the American teenage girl, and this meant that they were doomed. The smallest one probably thought she was too short, the other one too tall. The most beautiful one had no breasts, the buxom one had crisp thin hair.

My heart softened, and I could breathe again (although I would have killed for a sarong). I felt deep compassion for them; I wanted to tell them the good news—that at some point you give up on ever looking much better than you do. Somehow, you get a little older, a littler fatter, and you end up going a little easier on yourself. Or a lot easier. And I no longer felt ugly, maybe just a little ridiculous, I held my head a bit higher; I touched the aunties gently, to let them know I was there, and that made me less afraid. Ugliness is creeping around in fear, I remembered. Yet here I was, almost naked, and—to use the medical term—flabbier than shit, but deeply loyal to myself.

I forced myself not to check out their butts.

Finally, mercifully, a van came along and took us up the hill. The girls got off before me and walked toward their rooms. God—they had the most incredibly small butts. It made me want to kill myself.

When I got to my room, I took a long, hot shower and then stood studying myself naked in the mirror. I looked like Divine. But then I thought about the poor aunties, how awful it must feel to have me judging them so harshly—the darling aunties! A gasp at this injustice escaped my lips, and my heart grew soft and maternal, and then I said out loud, "God! I am so sorry," and the aunties tucked their heads down shyly, not knowing now if they were safe. "Oh, *mon Dieu*," I told them and then, "Oh, my dears." I put on my sexiest t-shirt, my cutest underpants, and I slathered rose-scented lotion on my legs, rubbing it in gently with the indignation of a mother who has rescued her daughter from school-yard bullies or the hands of the Philistines.

I put on a little light foundation, as if making up a friend, a tiny bit of blusher, and way too much mascara—there are times when nothing else will do. Sam barged in, sunburned and hungry and demanding that we go to the dining room right that second, but the aunties and I ignored him.

Because now we were putting up our hair.

"Why do you have to do that when I'm *starving* to death?"

He wouldn't understand: he looks like a cross between God and Cindy Crawford. And I don't understand entirely either. But I knew to put on my favorite earrings. I wasn't thinking that I looked awful and wanted to look like someone else; that is the point at which you can come dangerously close to female impersonation. I just remembered that sometimes you start with the outside and you get it right. You tend to your spirit through the body. It's polishing the healthy young skin of that girl who was here just a moment ago, who still lives inside. It's saying that sometimes maybe one looks a little pale and wan and wants to shine a little light on oneself. Then, when you're in that honoring place, it's almost like makeup becomes a form of light, just as on those days when a little cloud cover makes you really notice the sun's rays that come slanting through. Maybe the key is simply a wry fondness for the thing you're slapping this stuff onto, instead of a desire to disguise; so it's not that you're wearing a coat of paint, but a mantilla.

Anne Lamott is the author of several books, including the novels Rosie *and* Crooked Little Heart, *and the nonfiction works* Operating Instructions, Bird by Bird, *and* Traveling Mercies: Some Thoughts on Faith, *from which this story was excerpted. She lives in Northern California.*

DEBORAH CHANEY

All-Natural Herbal Girl

It's all in your head.

As I eagerly heaved my five massive bags of luggage aboard the thirty-eight-foot Ingrid sailing vessel moored in Vancouver, British Columbia, I had romantic thoughts about this cruise to San Francisco. Equipped with my box of fifty herbal remedies, for everything from seasickness to constipation, blank journals and writing pens, art supplies, self-help books, wet weather gear, and warm clothes, I was ready to go blue water sailing. I envisioned myself hoisting the sails, popping a couple of ginger tablets, and kicking back, while I gazed at the horizon and wrote in my journal or painted or read. Disillusionment was mine and a lovely friend she was.

My dream was to sail down the West Coast of North America to Mexico. I had read *The Perfect Storm* and *Godforsaken Sea.* I had done some dinghy sailing several years back. I felt ready for anything. My plan was to talk my way onto boats and crew in exchange for room and board. It would be free and it would be fun.

Captain Bob was a fifty-year-old computer programmer

who had been dreaming for eight years of sailing *Orythyia* south. We hooked up via a crew advertisement on the Internet, a week later meeting in person at a little restaurant in downtown Vancouver. When I found out he ate health food, I knew it was meant to be. Bob also found Owen, our third crew member, on the Internet. Owen was a twenty-two-year-old know-it-all, and professed to Bob, before we left, that he was immune to seasickness.

Our ten-day journey began as we headed southwest, out of the Strait of Juan de Fuca. We pitched uncomfortably back and forth in the swells as we motored out, the sun sparkling on the ocean, the sky clear, and dolphins leaping and playing at our bow. Despite the beautiful scenery, I found it difficult to adjust to the boat's movement. I sat ill at ease on deck, clasping a bottle of grapefruit seed extract I was using to purify my drinking water. Eating was not a welcome idea for me. As for Owen, he retched over the side on our first day out, and was not seen eating for most of the trip. Bob remained totally unaffected by the boat's continual motion and, during the trip, ate up nearly everything in sight, including all the frozen dinners I had pre-cooked the week before we left.

Sleep was challenging, if nearly impossible, that first night. The valerian root droplets I took for sleeping were ineffective. I was cold, the boat rocked too much, the rigging was too noisy, and the sound and feel of the cold black bottomless ocean rushing by gave me the chills. During numerous intervals of his night watch, from midnight until four A.M., Owen yelled down into the cabin waking Bob to ask him trivial questions about adjusting the sails. Eventually Bob leapt out of bed, cursing and swearing, and went up to help Owen. One hour later, Bob went back to bed and our first victim, the diesel heater, quit. Thick gray smoke filled the cabin. Bob woke up choking and coughing, cursing again, and ready to throttle Owen. He opened the top cabin hatch, the smoke cleared, and the cabin was now cold as ice. I wondered if there was a homeopathic remedy for this sleepless nightmare.

As we veered our course and headed south, the rhythm of life at sea took over. One day melted into the next. Owen did the cooking, I washed dishes, and Bob charted our course. We all took turns through the days and nights at four-hour watch shifts each, skippering the boat, keeping an eye out, and plotting our position. I spent my free time on deck, where I was less inclined to feel ill. I sat watching the horizon in realization that writing in my journal, painting, and reading were out of the question. I went down into the cabin only on occasion, to lather my body with aromatherapy oils, determined to ward off my ever-increasing bodily stench.

I loved the sacredness of sailing through the night. Billions of stars enveloped me, bright green phosphorescence glowing from our wake, and the beautiful silence of being out on my own was magical. Every night I watched the magnificent production of darkness fading to dusk, stars melting away, and the sun rising to join me.

Three days out, the engine decided to give up the ghost. Bob soon realized that all the tantrums and cuss words in the world wouldn't change a thing. No wind meant no way. Now with the diesel heater and the motor gone, we were lucky that the warm northwesterly winds kept up. We continued moving at an average of six knots.

On our fifth day, a storm started building. Owen was on watch and, as usual, he had woken Bob up several times earlier that night with his various petty concerns. However, this time Owen's concern was justified. During the early morning hours, the wind had picked up to forty knots and waves were raging at twelve feet. They woke me to help bring the boat heaved-to. I hurriedly pulled on my foul-weather gear while being thrown around like a rag doll in the cabin. Outside, I clipped in my lifeline, and felt the surge of wind and seawater being driven at me. Cold water seeped down my boots, soaking my dry, warm socks.

> Things are going to get a lot worse before they get worse.
>
> ◆
>
> —Lily Tomlin

I took watch that night during the storm. I checked the rigging and surrounding waters every twenty minutes until daybreak. It wasn't long before I knew I was close to vomiting. All I wanted to do was lie down. Bob and Owen had finally awoken. To their inquiries of my well-being, all I could muster was, "I need a bucket." The all-natural dried ginger tablets I had been so religiously taking were proving to be ineffective, seasickness having now taken her full course.

That next day I was in worse condition and unable to do any tasks to help out onboard. I lay on deck feeling sorry for myself, barely able to summon the effort to go down below to take my ginger tablets. Bob approached me. "Stop all this righteous herbal shit and put on the f'ing patch. Do this, or get off the boat." We were one hundred nautical miles from land. I decided to employ the patch. I used some medical tape to stick it behind my ear. When no one was looking, I popped a couple more ginger tablets.

Within the several hours of its application, the patch had taken its effect and I was now super patch woman. I could do anything! I was preparing meals, writing in my journal, and even reading books. Thank God for pharmaceuticals, I thought, smiling inwardly.

Three days later I peeled off the patch. Half an hour into "normal" drug-free existence, Bob came up on deck holding my patch and laughing. Apparently I had not put it on correctly. The plastic cover was still in place. I couldn't believe it! All that time I had thought that I was super patch woman but really I was still the all-natural herbal girl!

On the ninth day, the wind vein collapsed and the wind decided to quit simultaneously. We were sixty miles off San Francisco Bay, no diesel heater, no motor, no wind vein, and now, no wind. It was dead calm and the cease in motion was a welcome feeling. I tossed off my clothes, dived into the ocean and began to scrub my filthy body. After watching dubiously, the boys caught on and jumped in as well. A couple of hours later the wind picked up and we sailed east to San Francisco. Later, as the streets of Sausalito rose and fell beneath me, I wondered if there was an herbal remedy for acclimatizing back to land.

When she is not out adventuring, Deborah Chaney works as a freelance writer as well as doing odd jobs to put bread on the table. She is currently working on her first book, a motivational title for young women. See her work at www.DEBCreative.com

ELLEN DEGENERES

The Plane Truth

It's another world up there.

I KNOW THAT THE EXPERTS SAY YOU'RE MORE LIKELY to get hurt crossing the street than you are flying (these, of course, would be the street-crossing experts), but that doesn't make me feel any less frightened of flying. If anything, it makes me more afraid of crossing the street. As soon as the light turns green, I run across the street as fast as I can, screaming like a madwoman. I arrive on the other side out of breath, wheezing, and clutching my stomach (or if I'm in a whimsical mood, the stomach of the person standing next to me).

So, to conquer my fear of flying, I decided to write down my feelings on a recent trip. I kept an in-flight journal (which is like an in-flight movie—but without anyone standing up in front of you so you miss the good parts, and with better sound).

I felt edgy the moment I stepped into the aircraft. That could be why I snapped at the woman in front of me. In my defense, she did ask the flight attendant a pretty stupid question: "Excuse me, where is seat 27-B?" I mean, really. But I see now that I overreacted when I screamed at her, "Well, moron you walk in the only direction you can, and it's the 27th row seat B—next to seat A. All righty?!" That sort of response is probably one of the many reasons why I'm not a flight attendant.

It was only when the woman (27-B) turned around to look at me that I saw she was a nun. I guess that sort of hat-like thing she wore on her head should have given me a clue, but sometimes I don't have that good an eye for details.

I tried to apologize by smiling and giving her a playful punch on the arm to let her know I was joking. Well, either my playful punch carried more of a wallop than I intended (due to the tension I feel about flying), or her advanced years made her frailer than she appeared, or she was just a big old ham (which is my theory), but the nun shouted out, "Owww!" and rubbed her arm like she was in pain. She rolled up her sleeve and...you know, that bruise could *easily* have been there before I hit her.

My good friend Jasmine (at least I think that's her name; I'm so scared that it's affecting my already rattled memory; I know that it's the name of a tea, so if it's not Jasmine, it's either Earl Grey or Hibiscus) told me that a good way to combat fear is to chant. So all the way to my seat I was chanting, "I'm going to die, I'm going to die, oh sweet Lord, I'm going to die." It didn't work. If anything, I was more petrified when I got to my seat (27-A). Even seeing the familiar face of the nun in 27-B (who seemed to flinch when she saw me) didn't calm me down.

So here I am, sitting in my seat, working on my journal. Hey, there's a fly on this plane. I am so scared of flying, I can't imagine how flies do it all day, every day. But, then again, that's what a fly does, fly. It's his job. What's going through that fly's mind? He's looking out the window and probably saying to himself, "Wow, look how high up I am. I've never gotten up this high, I am going very, very fast, and I'm not really working any harder than I usually do."

This fly just happened to wander onto a plane in Los Angeles. Several hours later it is going to get off in New York, but more in a *Home Alone 2* kind of way.

A bunch of flies will probably be waiting as it gets off the plane. They'll all be hugging, blocking the way. Nobody will get by. There will even be a chauffeur holding a tiny sign that says FLY. I'll be relieved to see he has friends there. Well, I'm assuming it's a *he*. It's so hard to tell unless you hold them really still and look closely, and I don't want do that on the plane with people around. That's something you should do at home—alone.

Aghhhhhh! What was that? "Fuck, we're going to crash!!!"

Oh, I wish I hadn't shouted that out loud. It was just the beverage cart rumbling by. Being on a plane just freaks me out. Any little movement, and suddenly it's like I have Tourette's syndrome. Anything at all—"Fuck! Shit!" I don't even curse. I never curse. It's so embarrassing. "Pardon me, Sister, I am sorry, I...I was frightened. Pray for me."

Now she's going to turn on that little air thing above her. Maybe I'm paranoid, but I think it takes power away from the plane somehow. I get mad if people next to me use theirs.

"Sister, don't use that, that's...Dang! Shut it off! I'll hit ya! Shut it off!!"

The nun just left to find a different seat. Some people are so touchy. I'm sure she didn't learn that little hand gesture in her convent, either.

As scary as this flight is, it's nothing compared to those tiny Buddy Holly planes that I've had to fly in to get to different stand-up performances. Oh God, those little propeller planes, those little eight-seater tiny planes where you can actually see the pilots in the cockpit. They're reading through some manuals like *So You Want to Be a Pilot.* They're just flipping through the pamphlet trying to figure out which buttons to push to land the plane.

I've got to relax somehow. Why didn't I think of this sooner? I'll recline my seat. Oh, that makes all the difference. That $^{3}/_{4}$ of an inch between upright and reclined is the difference between agony and ecstasy. I never thought $^{3}/_{4}$ of an inch could mean so much. *Now* I can sleep. When I get home, I'm going to put some gizmo in my chairs so that they go back $^{3}/_{4}$ of an inch, too. I wouldn't overdo it like the guy sitting in front of me. His seat goes so far back that his head is practically in my lap. I can pretty much read his newspaper.

I'd better not get too comfortable in my $^{3}/_{4}$-of-an-inch recline because toward the end of the flight, the flight attendant is going to say, "You're going to have to put your seat in the upright position for landing." They're so adamant about that every single time, like that's gonna make a difference. Because if we crash, the investigators are going to say, "Oh, that's a shame, her seat was reclined $^{3}/_{4}$ of an inch. When will they learn? What was that—30,000 feet? She could have made that. Sheesh. If only she'd been upright."

Being reclined isn't working. I'm still freaking out. I know what I need. "Oh, flight attendant. Oh, ma'am." You have to talk nice to the flight attendants because they're all arrogant little bitches. Unless, of course, you happen to be a flight attendant or are related to or are friends with one—then you are the absolutely lovely exceptions to this rule. But the rest of them, they have this attitude. And they can afford to have the attitude, because they have the power—they have the peanuts.

They have these six peanuts that we need. Six peanuts. Somebody could offer that to you on the street, and you'd say, "I don't want that shit—get that away from me. Six peanuts? No-oh." Somehow they've done research. They know that the higher we go, the more we need nuts. And we go crazy if we don't get them.

"Miss, I didn't get my, uh—my peanuts. And I'd really appreciate it if you gave me some. They're good, aren't they? I've never been able to get them on the ground either. At least not ones this good. Thank you. Oh, thank you."

Fuck, what was that! "We're going to crash!" Oops, false alarm. It's just the food cart coming down the aisle.

I think they only give you six peanuts so that you don't spoil your appetite for the disgusting meal that's soon to follow. You never hear anybody say, "You know, I can't finish that. Could you wrap that up for me please? That was delicious. It's just too much, I'm stuffed! What was that, pigeon?"

But we do get excited about it, don't we? "Oh, here comes the cart, put down the tray! La la la la. Put down your tray! They're starting on the other side first. Hurry! Hurry! Those people over there—they're eating. Those people are eating."

This is the tiniest food I've ever seen in my entire life. I guess they figure everything's relative. You get that high up, you look out the window, "Well, it's as big as that house down there. I can't eat all that. Look at the size of that. It's as big as a house. Me thinking I could eat all that! Ha! Split that steak with me. Now *that's* a steak." Any kind of meat that you get—chicken, steak, anything—has grill marks on each side, like somehow we'll actually believe there's an open-flame grill in the front of the plane.

Salads are always two pieces of dead lettuce and salad dressing that comes in that astronaut package. As soon as you open it, it's on your neighbor's lap. "Could I just dip my lettuce, ma'am? Hm, that's a lovely skirt. What is that, silk?" But you know, should that happen, club soda's gonna get that stain out immediately.

That's the answer to anything you ask up there, I don't know if you've noticed that.

"Excuse me, I have an upset stomach."
"Club soda, be right back."
"Excuse me, I spilled something."
"Club soda, be right back."
"Ooh, the wing is on fire!"
"Club soda, be right back."

I thought the food would make me feel less frightened. But it didn't. Maybe if I stretch my legs and go to the restroom it will help.

That was the tiniest bathroom I've ever been in. I guess they figure since the food is so tiny, the bathrooms should be minuscule, too. I read a book once where two people had sex in an airplane bathroom. I don't see how that's possible. I barely had enough room to sit down. There is a lit sign in there that reads: "Return to Seat. Return to Cabin." Why do they think that needs to be lit? Because we'll relax in there for a little while? "Miss, bring my peanuts in here, please. This is *beautiful*. The water is so blue, it reminds me of the Mediterranean. I don't ever want to leave."

You have no concept of time when you're in there—it's like a casino: no windows, no clocks. I could be the only one to get up out of my seat to go to the bathroom—everybody else is sound asleep when I go—but after I've been in there for what I think is thirty seconds, I open the door and everyone in the plane is lined up, looking at their watches, making me feel like I've been in there forever.

And now I've got to explain the smell that was in there

before I went in there. Does that ever happen to you? It's not your fault. You've held your breath, you just wanna get out, and now you open the door and you have to explain, "Oh! Listen, there's an odor in there and I didn't do it. It's bad. You might want to sprinkle some club soda, if you uh..."

I think my only hope of escaping my mind-numbing fear is to sleep; to sleep and perchance to dream. The only trouble is when I fall asleep on a plane, I always have a nightmare....

Ellen Degeneres is a stand-up comedian, has hosted the Emmy and the Grammy Awards, and has starred in two sitcoms, Ellen *and* The Ellen Show, *as well as three Hollywood films. Recipient of the American Comedy Award, she has penned a humorous book,* My Point...And Do I Have One, *from which this story was excerpted.*

*

Early the next morning I took the wheel of our bed in a shed. Suddenly, I was Columbus. I was Lewis & Clark. I was Huck Finn with AAA maps. Look out territory, here we come! But that first turn out of suburbia is a trickster and a shower of Legos, ketchup, sodas, and shampoo crashed down on the floor in the back half of the RV. Our kids, seated in the midst of the ruckus, thought this was great entertainment. My husband peeled himself off the roof of the truck cab. I headed for the nearest café.

And then I drove and drove and drove. Not because I am the road mama I imagine myself to be, but because I really couldn't stop. I was terrified to change lanes, much less veer toward an exit. My hands were white-knuckled into a permanent grip on the steering wheel. I couldn't see over the hood of the beast, there was no rear-view mirror, the side-view mirrors were too far away, and the cars around me were too close. The whole thing was noisy as a school bus full of third-graders and felt like a top-heavy trash truck on a windy day. I wasn't Huck anymore. I was Jonah in the belly of the big fish. In short, I was freaking out.

—Dawn Bonker, "Bed in a Shed"

CHRISTINE NIELSEN

Sand in My Bra

She put on her high-heeled sneakers
and went out to burn the man.

I HAD JUST COMPLETED MY FOURTH TO-DO LIST WHEN it occurred to me that all these lists might just end up eating me alive. I stared at the tasks that stood between me and my week of absolute freedom, a week of what I knew would be amazing fun: sleeping bag, tent, flashlight, dust masks, water, goggles, body paint, baby wipes (substitute for showering in the desert), food for ten days, costumes. Costumes. One little word, and yet it was staring at me with daunting intensity. I was heading off in less than a week to be part of a community based on creative self-expression and I knew I couldn't arrive in jeans and a t-shirt. I needed to find some clothes to express my inner something-or-other.

Determined, I jumped in my car and headed to thrift stores and costume shops. A ticket to Burning Man is a ticket that enables you to finally wear that wedding dress and blue wig combo you've been dreaming about. You can finally be a roller-skating disco diva, and it's not even Halloween. Four stores, six hours, and 100 bucks later, I arrived home, exuberant with my purchases.

I organized my elaborate dresses into one pile, my sequined and sparkly stuff in another, and my black fake leather and fishnets in yet another. I threw in two wigs, some jewelry (including disco-ball earrings), a few feet of faux fur, a pair of ballet slippers, and a cape. Now, all I had to do was locate twenty gallons of water, supports for a shade structure, a spray bottle, and a bike. No time to let the endless flow of lists stop me now. In just a few short days, I would be ready for the desert, ready for Burning Man.

This crazy celebration of life's diversity and creativity began in San Francisco in 1986 when a man named Larry Harvey and a few of his friends built an effigy of a man and burned it on Baker Beach in honor of the summer solstice, innovative art, and the pirating of land. In a few short years, this tradition grew into an event that required space—so much more space, in fact, that the event was relocated to Black Rock Desert, Nevada. Over the twelve years that it has called this endless, empty expanse its home, Burning Man has evolved into a temporary city of more than 25,000 people, making it the most populous town in the entire county for that week. The bustling city boasts thriving boulevards and avenues lined with flames for night vision, two daily newspapers, more than twenty radio stations, fully equipped and competent medical volunteers, a fire department, an airport, a department of Public Works, and even a DMV (Department of Mutant Vehicles). Creating something from nothing, every single Black Rock City citizen participates in the building and subsequent clean-up of this phenomenal artistic experiment.

As we finally approached the Black Rock Desert playa, a prehistoric dried-up lakebed, I thought back to all the fond memories I had of this place. Of naked green men riding unicycles and chanting praises to pizza. Of parades of red people chanting the praises of red. I remembered the trip I took on a fire-breathing dragon that had a five-piece polka band on board. I remembered the alien space ship I danced in all night. I thought of the faces of the sweet people I'd met. I thought of the possibilities of this year—of fire and water and dust. The anticipation made my hair stand on end.

My friends and I were greeted at the gate by a man in pants made of teddy bears, a woman reliving her days as a Catholic schoolgirl (or perhaps reinventing those days in a more grown-up way), and a guy who was best described as a desert rat. (This is a name of honor that longtime desert and Burning Man dwellers give themselves. They can best be identified by the copious amounts of playa dust covering every inch of their bodies.) As we approached, we rolled down our windows and the schoolgirl knelt down.

"Are you a virgin?" she asked coyly, eyes directed at me.

For a moment I was insulted by such a personal question until I remembered what the question meant: Am I a Burning Man virgin?

"No!" I said proudly.

She offered me a sweet smile and said, "Welcome back home."

She then turned her attention to my friend, her eyes implying the same question. My friend, looking a little nervous, sheepishly replied, "Yes."

Upon hearing this, the schoolgirl jumped for joy and screamed, "We've got a virgin!" and yanked open our car door. Outside, all three greeters congregated. My friend was still sitting behind the wheel, unsure if she should get out, or perhaps put the car in reverse and get out of there.

"We need you to sing a song!" the teddy bear pants guy said.

"What song?" she asked.

"How about your ABCs?" the schoolgirl squealed.

They were all so excited for this rendition of the alphabet song that I couldn't help but giggle, despite my friend's obvious nervousness. She started out quiet and unsure, but by about L, the volume was increasing, as was everyone's enthusiasm, and by P, everyone was screaming, not singing, along. By the Z grand finale, my friend was hugging and slapping five to our greeters, and they all welcomed her home.

And that's what the Black Rock Desert playa would be to us for the next ten days—home.

Since participation is key at Burning Man, I was proud to be part of a giant theme camp and the first few days of my stay I helped build it. The camp was an enormous playground consisting of a trampoline, a swing set, two rickety slides that I refused to go on, a 3-D Twister game, and a geodesic dome. Somewhere around mid-week, our foreman, a genius/madman, approached me and said something like this: "Christine, I need you to go collect some 8 x 10s, drill holes in them, and connect them with zip ties to the infrastructure of the tubular PVC tubing, and then perpendicularly hatch them from the third scaffolding layer to the rebar joints in the front of camp, okay? You can use my mega-watt electrical power-bit drill—that'll make it easier."

The heat had made him crazy, I concluded, and I realized that I needed to get out of camp. I needed some action that didn't require PVC piping or nails. My friend Doug and I jumped on our vehicles, our bikes (vehicles are as diverse here as baby carriages and pirate ships), and fled the scene. A bike to a Burning Man-goer is as essential as a handbag to a chic city woman. You simply cannot leave home without one. The endless space combined with the elements of heat (110 degrees is nothing), wind, and dust instantly kick anyone's ass who thinks they can brave the expanse on foot.

Besides the heat, Burning Man thrives on four things: community, participation, self-expression, and self-reliance. Beyond these core values, which keep the event running, there are no rules (save the rules to protect the health and safety of other participants and the land). Thus, it is a mecca where creativity and self-expression can run wild. Endless desert spaces make it ideal for huge art installations and interactive art pieces. Another unique aspect of Burning Man is that it runs almost entirely on a gift economy. There are precisely two things the U.S. dollar will buy you: bags of ice and coffee. For anything else, your money has about as much value as a square of toilet paper. So, instead of seeing cash registers and advertisements (ads are not allowed at Burning Man), you see mad professors trading watermelon for a foot massage and cowboys performing the Macarena for a cold can of beer. If you can imagine it, it has a place at Burning Man.

Our biking adventure began as we circled the roller rink, which proudly boasted disco to die for. I silently thanked the Burning Man gods for proving that disco lives on. We continued past the DMV, past the soul-shaking beats of Taiko drumming camp, past the larger-than-life Connect Four Board and towering Lite-Brite. I saw a Santa Claus handing out candy, a marching band parade, a vehicle that threw flames, and a group of women who looked like they were heading for prom.

It was mid-afternoon and the sun was relentless by the time we came across a little piece of heaven. It was a big-rig truck that lured us in with its name: Antarctica. Inside was other-worldly. Here in the middle of the desert, in the middle of an excruciatingly hot day, I was suddenly cold. Not just chilly cold, but goose bumps cold. I looked around to discover images of polar bears, icebergs, penguins, and snow flashing on the inside of this semi.

It was a meat-packing truck. This was how the good people of America received their fresh meat, and here we were, turning it into the coolest party on the playa. Hard-hitting DJ music roared out of the truck and wannabe Eskimos grooved inside with the biggest smiles on their faces. It was the best party I'd found so far—Antarctica, right here in the Nevada desert!

After we'd had our fill of Antarctic air, Doug and I decided to head back to camp. On our way, we gave a second look at what seemed the craziest mirage we'd seen yet. It wasn't a water mirage, it wasn't a fire breathing pirate ship mirage, or even a floating rubber duckie mirage. It was something much stranger than those things. It was a cubicle, an honest-to-god office cubicle, complete with a fax machine, a computer, a desk chair, and a sign posting workers' rights. It was the strangest thing I saw all week. After confirming its reality, Doug and I fled from it in hushed confusion.

When the trauma passed, my mind began to focus on something much more important: my playa wardrobe. A man dressed as a jellyfish bobbed up and down beside me and I looked down to realize I was wearing a stupid khaki skirt and a black tank top. I took another look at the walking marine man. His outfit towered over his shoulders, beautiful incandescent strips of pink and purple flowing over his head and down his back. I was swimming in a sea of creatures and I was mere khaki sea slime.

Considering the amount of time and energy I had put into Burning Man clothes, I had envisioned myself out on the playa stopping traffic with my creative outfits. I intended to be an outer space diva, little green riding hood, a southern belle, and a disco desert chic all in the same week. Maybe even all in the same day. I brought enough clothes with me to justify changing outfits at least six times daily. I even brought a full-length mirror to put in my tent.

So, of course, once I got settled I realized I had nothing to wear. I pored over my clothes for at least an hour, trying on, taking off, throwing in a corner, and again. I couldn't make anything work. I was given ultimate freedom to dress however I liked, to be whomever I pleased, and it seemed that the freedom was too much for me to handle. Frustrated, I left the heat of my tent in that same khaki skirt.

I needed a Bloody Mary.

I found my friend Charly and a few minutes later I had a deliciously cool cocktail in my hands. Sipping my drink and gazing around my surroundings, I once again grew anxious to explore. Surely there were fire-eating men and fire-breathing women to be seen! I mustn't miss it! A blue naked guy walked by hula hooping as he took each step, and I decided that would be my sign to be on my way. Boring outfit and all, I jumped on my bike again.

As I cruised my mind drifted again to just how cool everyone looked but me. Furry suits, sequined halter tops, tiaras, leather chaps, evening gowns. Fishnet stockings, elaborate red wings, and white flowing skirts. Damn, I thought, as each woman passed. Why hadn't I thought of that? Mental notes were overflowing. In fact, I was so deep in the land of mental notes and Bloody Mary (yes, it's true, I was drinking and driving—well, riding) that I almost had a head-on collision with an angel. She appeared out of nowhere and I just about ran her over. But I stopped just short and before I could even attempt an apology, she was offering me the best present I had had out on the playa—cantaloupe. In Black Rock City, on a day that *must* be over 110 degrees, cantaloupe is not a mere fruit. When you have been riding your bike and inhaling bags of dust, your mouth feels like the face of the desert itself, and cantaloupe spelled r-e-l-i-e-f. It was the best possible gift.

Inspired by the fruit and beverage refreshments, I decided to head back to my tent where I was determined to emerge a Burning Man beauty. On my way back to camp, I stopped at Floss Camp. Free floss, a mirror, a trash can, and room to write the praises of flossing, all at your disposal. I set the tomato juice and cantaloupe free from my mouth, which gave me the illusion of having clean teeth, and I went on my way.

Clean though my gums may have believed themselves to be, in reality any thought of being clean at Burning Man is an illusion. There is nowhere that the pesky playa dust can't find you (this thought makes me cringe every time I see a naked body wandering about). Those who take showers are sorely disappointed when they take their first step out of the makeshift camp shower. Squish. Squish. Wet foot meets playa in a phenomenon known as the all-natural instant platform look. Fresh with this newest style in footwear, these poor souls dry off with a playa-dusty towel. My advice? Learn to love the dust because it's not going anywhere but all over you.

Back at camp again, the buzz was no longer about Antarctica. Now the talk was all Critical Tits. Yes, Critical Tits, one of the most important events at Burning Man: 4,000 women, 8,000 breasts, one huge parade. Based on the San Francisco tradition Critical Mass, Critical Tits is also a huge annual bike ride. But while the ride in San Francisco focuses on bikers' rights, this one focuses on the beauty of breasts.

Even without a watch, I realized I had no time to spare if I wanted to be in the parade. So, my top came off, and my khaki skirt and I charged bravely out once again! As my friends and I rode topless on our bikes, I was blown away at the mass of people in front of me. It was the largest single gathering I'd seen yet at Burning Man. As we got closer, I was engulfed in a sea of topless women—women of all shapes, sizes, ages, and ethnicities. Large women, short women, crazy and loud women, quiet and reserved women, straight women, gay women, skinny women, even pregnant women. Double Ds, miniature As. You name it, I saw it. I imagined the everyday lives of these women. I imagined everything from front girl in a punk band to investment banker on Wall Street. Moms with their daughters, college students, artists, intellectuals. Painted breasts and plain breasts alike were welcome on the parade route. Some women were intricately decorated, with vibrant colors and dazzling sparkles. Some women had doo-dads hanging off their nipples—plastic goldfish and dangling beads.

I was shooting a basket from the free throw line when somebody yelled, "Naked Basketball!" There were cheers of agreement and I went into a coma. Just like our first day of orientation for this bike trip when someone got the bright idea for us all to shave our heads. I was frozen, numb, and if there was a mirror in that place, a thousand bucks says I had my hands covering my chest with my legs crossed, all curled up in the fetal position, eyes closed, and singing as loud as I could, "la la la la la la la la la."

—Jennifer L. Leo, "Breasts"

The strength of our crowd drowned out any lingering embarrassment of our bare-breasted attire. Even the seemingly shy women were unabashed and proud. Energy and pride overflowed on the parade route, and I laughed to myself as I heard someone from the sidelines yell, "God bless Critical Tits! God bless Critical Tits!"

It was, shall we say, a peak experience, as we were gathering for the simple occasion of celebrating our femaleness in its most elemental form. We were celebrating our boobies!

Two hours, a parade, and a party later, I was ready for more clothes. It was also starting to get dark. As everyone applauded the sunset, and the lamplighters made their daily trek to light the city streets, I too prepared for the night.

I finally shed the khaki skirt and transformed into the Burning Man Diva I was always meant to be, then headed out and cruised along the playa, stars above and dust below, in a giant squid mutant vehicle. Suddenly a man wearing djinni-style pants came running trying to catch up with me.

"Stop! Stop!" he yelled with intensity.

I looked back, a bit confused.

"The sultan! The sultan!"

Now I was even more confused. The sultan?

"The sultan wishes to see you, the sultan demands your presence—please, get off that giant squid and follow me. This is indeed a matter of grave importance!"

As I followed the man back to an elaborately decorated tent, he explained to me what an honor this was—the sultan did not wish to see just anyone. I ducked through the entrance of softly flowing fabric into what was indeed a sultan's palace. I slowly raised my eyes, and there he was. The sultan.

He sat bejeweled high up on intricately adorned pillows. I sank to my knees. "I need your help," he said in a deep sultany voice. "Please, come forward."

I approached him on my knees until I was in front of him. I was impressed with the amount of riches all around me.

"I'll do what I can," I told him.

"Very well. I need you to tell me what the capital of Montana is. It's a matter of grave importance. Really."

Of all the questions. Montana. I thought, head down, nervous as all eyes were on me. Think...think....think...all the way back to tenth grade geography....

"Helena?" I replied.

"She's right! My God, I think she's right!" the sultan exclaimed. "My child, you have no idea what sort of good you have created here!" Everyone in the tent cheered.

He was right, I did have no idea what was so important about Helena, or what I had created. All I knew was that when I had answered correctly, the sultan draped a few strands of gold beads around my neck and took my hand to raise me up. Then he suddenly stopped speaking in his grandiose sultan voice, told me his name was Bob, and offered me a beer. I thanked him, took a cushioned seat, and watched as more people were summoned.

When I had had my fill of living a royal life, I thanked Sultan Bob and once again set out into the desert. The stars were shining brightly and the air was cool. I was feeling great. I had made my transformation—finally—from the boring khaki skirt girl to little green riding hood—complete with disco ball earrings. I felt like a desert goddess.

Thinking of all the beautiful people I'd seen that day and all the adventures I'd had, I purposefully strode across the vast expanse of the desert, heading toward beats I knew would make me groove. The moon was directly above and I was free, free, free. I smiled to myself, knowing that I still had four more days to go.

Christine Nielsen has explored many regions of this earth, but one of her favorite destinations will always be Burning Man. Her current project is taking her to South America to promote women's heath education.

KATHLEEN MEYER

* * *

Sometimes a Great Myth

Travel isn't as much about where *you go as where you* go.

DURING THE HOARY, FLASH-FREEZING MONTHS OF A long Montana winter, things can close in, suffocate you, rearrange your brain cells. It was mid-January, when it happened to me—still the dark days and showing no promise of thaw. I was talking on the phone with Harvey Partner, manufacturer of the JON-NY PARTNER, a bomb-proof, stainless steel box used by river runners and horse packers for transporting human excretions (the brown solid stuff, for the most part) out of the backcountry and delivering it to civilization where it can be properly treated. Partner's portable toilet—one of about a dozen similarly purposed contraptions—emerged on the outdoor equipment scene for two reasons: in general, as a response to the explosion in the number of visitors to wild places; in specific, to comply with a newfangled EPA ruling. The JON-NY PARTNER is considered the Cadillac of its ilk. It is equipped with carrying handles and a toilet seat with lid and a hose-and-funnel clean-out apparatus that is compatible with RV dumping stations. Were the holding tank to catapult out of a raft into the mother of all rapids and bash onto every rock in the river, it more than likely would not toss its innards. Gathering specifics on this contraption was part of the ground work for compiling the second edition of my book, *How to Shit in the Woods: An Environmentally Sound Approach to a Lost Art*. A task in which I was deeply immersed.

"How large of a holding tank," I asked, "would be required for two weeks?"

"Depends on the group and what they're eating," Partner said, expounding on how he had the canister tested with a commercial outfitter for a full season on the Grand Canyon of the Colorado River. "We wanted a good cross section of people on a diet they'd get on a river trip, like pork chops and omelets for breakfast. Turns out, the species *Homo sapiens* on a stout diet requires carry-out capacity of twenty-seven cubic inches per day." To be precise. "Some folks will put more in there than others, but that's the average."

I quickly began to calculate, conjuring up a fancy turd compactor that could square a lump to 3" x 3" x 3". I was desperate—God knows, for some reason—to learn whether I fell within the parameters of "average."

"So, how many of these holding tanks," I pressed him, "would be needed for, say, a thirty-person, fourteen-day trip?"

"Let's see. Four hundred and twenty man-days divided by…"

"*Person*-days, Harv," I teasingly corrected him. Protracted conversation on the topic of excrement serves to kick out the foundation blocks of professional stiffness.

He began again, this time slowly and with crisp enunciation to every word. "Four hundred and twenty *asshole-days* divided by sixty per box." I heard the ratchety click of a calculator. "Seven boxes."

Seven boxes! I envisioned a raft with no passengers, one

piled with gear, a rig outfitters assign to green guides for practice rowing—only this one was loaded to the oarlocks with poo. A honey raft! The world had changed beyond all imagining.

Out in the wilds, enjoying that invigorating feeling of being away from people, you take a deep breath and that smell reaches you nostrils; that smell or a vision of a brown deposit—or worse—the realization you've just stepped in it. It just spoils your moment, your day. But maybe the poor unfortunate who left the deposit had nowhere else to "go." It's a problem, isn't it? Or is it? Actually it is not so difficult to dispose of your offerings responsibly. Ideally your turd should be buried in the top six to eight inches of organic soil, and covered with six inches of dirt.

—Dr. Jane Wilson-Howarth, *Shitting Pretty*

For several weeks this subject, which seems to be overwhelmingly mine, had never let up. By phone, e-mail, letter, and fax, it dogged me. Even followed me to bed with My Sweet Loverman. One afternoon we are going down for a nap, each thinking to read a bit. But I soon pull the downy coverlet up to my chin, with my head sinking into the pillow, and sigh, "I think I'm too tired to read."

"Does my Arctic Blossom want to be read to? Would she like to hear twenty pithy maxims?" His is a wry-witted humor, and he is reading the *Whole Earth Review*.

"Hmm, what do you mean maxims?" I ask, trying to ascertain if I'll be at all interested, but dropping off fast.

"Pithy maxims? Oh, I think they're sort of like high-fiber turds."

A moment of silence, peals of laughter.

Holed up in the marginally heated old barn we call home, to stay warm in winter I don five or six layers of clothing. I cut more the figure of the Pillsbury Dough Boy than the beleaguered Thumbelina I was lately feeling: a wee being fallen into an infinitely vast vat of crud, riding great whorls down a sucking vortex. Truth be known, the moniker "Shit Lady" is no big deal. Yet being a person infatuated with the glop is quite another story, one flatly at odds with even the most far-flung of the self-images I've nurtured over the years. If I were to sit down and tally up my fecal-absorbed hours, beyond a doubt there would be interest from the Guinness Book of Records. More and more, with the snowdrifts piling up, the walls heaving inward, there came lurking a naked question: Could I be obsessed?

Pervertedly so?

I mean, what would you say to a person who didn't seem able to go anywhere, do anything, that didn't eventually lapse into an interlude on the topic of elimination? It's O.K. deary, it's probably just your English heritage, the great-grandmother on your mother's side, you know, the stern one in all the dusty pictures? Everyone knows the English are preoccupied with their sinkers and floaters. It was, after all, the Englishman Thomas Crapper who bequeathed to the world, not only the flush toilet, but so illustrious a word as his surname.

As obsessions go, a rapt involvement with fecal matter probably wouldn't boot a person to the top of the unhealthy hierarchy. But an obsession is an obsession, shit no exception. I wasn't positive there weren't untold circles of hell ahead for a person so possessed. Shit converser today, coprophagist tomorrow?

To this last, a familiar inner voice reared up in defense. *Get off it! If it were flowers, you wouldn't think yourself besotted—you'd be the Tulip or the Hollyhock Lady and puzzle not at the hours they consume.* True enough. Yet, I was acutely aware of a propensity I had for confusing *defending* and *defensive.*

In Montana's hinterlands, you can burn up a tankerload of petroleum looking for a good therapist or applicable twelve-step program. Life has its conundrums when you are at once a Montanan, an advocate of living gently on the planet, and a quivering wreck fearful of having become an addict of a bizarre type. Out here, health becomes a balancing act. You harness your craziness to harrowing, haying, feeding, hoeing. Or during the howling snows of winter, you (no kidding, everyone and their cousins) turn to writing—another of the great obsessive pursuits. The trick lies in not allowing a particular wrinkle to consume you.

Was I harnessed, then, or off the deep end? Judging from my mail there were enough shit-conversers strung around the planet to found several chapters of Ca-Ca Anonymous. Grasping for an immediate solution, I settled on an old standby. Blowing town. We would get away from it all, flee to warm seas and the strains of Mariachi music. Travel, a little adventure, surely held the cure.

The last time my mate or I traipsed south of the border was long before we met, before ozone depletion, skin cancer scares, and AIDS. We were single then, wayward, rash, loosey-goosey. It was an era when America's youth fled to Mazatlan, Puerto Vallarta, Manzanillo, to seek true love in the sand, drink mescal and swallow the worm, dance into the sunrise, and, for those of us pale of skin, bake bodies to a shade that struck envy in the hearts of Caucasian friends. But in thirty years, things had changed. The world was different, Mexico was different, we were different.

Our plan was to set out overland in my old Ford pickup, park it in El Paso, and walk across the border to where we could hop public transportation and leisurely travel, pueblo to pueblo, as far south as a month would allow. The infinite wisdom in this plan stemmed from Honey Bucket's notion (a leftover perhaps from his hitchhiking days, or owning every edition of Carl Franz's *People's Guide to Mexico)* that when you travel by ground, you arrive with a notebook full of information on the place you've gotten to. Five days of blizzards, black ice, and cascading slush from passing semis, however, saw us only to Albuquerque. Notebooks blank, humors sprung. Then upon reaching El Paso, we discovered Mexican trains had recently dispensed with Pullman cars. Here, my dear one's resolve caved in, and we lucked onto bargain airline tickets for the big capital.

> Travel, they say, broadens the mind but in my experience it is the other end of the anatomy that feels the effect.
>
> —Beatrice Lillie

Now for a blast of irony. Before, yes *before*, we slipped south over the border, at our last stop, a restaurant in Las Cruses, New Mexico—from a plate of poblano chiles rellenos—Dear Heart contracted a case of traveler's trots. (It is necessary to note here this man is a health nut beyond all reason; he would sooner drink cod liver oil neat than poison his body with professionally prescribed medicine or even a couple of teeny-weeny over-the-counter pills. Therefore, much to his chagrin, and my consternation, he never managed to shake this plague until after having fully absorbed four days of U.S. food upon our return.) From another perturbed quarter, I swore I hear my faithful old subject—ears perked, tail wagging—pattering along our back trail.

By the time we made Oaxaca, I was jigging my own *turista* two-step. We were ensconced in Casa Arnel, a sweetly shabby, family-run *posada*, two stories constructed around a square central garden of tropical flowers and loud parrots, and eternally busy Mexican women tending chores. Laundry, strung on lines around the rooftop, cast fluttering shadows onto a pair of open-air dining tables, where shifts of German, Swiss, and American travelers chatted daylong over the dregs of the morning's *café*. Charming was the scene, yet with bowels and bodily functions having become the hourly topic of concern, we were two outdoor people feeling unduly cloistered. What's more, if we weren't quite old farts on the ever-curtaining stage of Life, we were certainly auditioning for the leading roles—more or less finished our drinking days, definitely concluded our drugging, fairly forgotten how to dance. Now, with Montezuma's Revenge in the director's chair, it was our empty-stomached mornings we cherished for sojourns, energies waning with the first bite of lunch. Then back to the *posada*.

Our lodgings, in the full gamut for tourists, were unassuming and tucked in a corner on the ground floor. A metal door and casement window fronted a small kitchen, furnished with a two-person table draped in kitschy red-flowered plastic, a two-burner countertop stove with green legs, a concrete sink, and a few shelves holding an assortment of Mexican crockery, cheap utensils, and aluminum cookware—though we weren't cooking. Just beyond, one step up, lay the bed chamber. During our now roughly all-afternoon napping sessions, we stretched naked in the oppressive heat on a board-hard bed overlaid with a thin cotton spread of dazzling blue, green, pink, yellow, and purple stripes. The Venetian blind on the window opposite was a throwback to the pastel décor of an earlier era: stripes of peach, baby blue, and lima bean green, four slats to the color. The walls were freshly painted a rich salmon color and the tile floor laid helter-skelter in vermilion swirl, solid cobalt blue, and one afterthought row of flesh tone (untanned). All in all, it was quaintly garish enough for me to love, but on a bad stomach it made my head swim.

Under the circumstances, we were overjoyed to have a private bathroom. The entirety of it—a doorless closet, equipped with sink and seatless commode—was actually a shower. Spray from the shower head arced in a pattern such that towels and toilet paper required removal during bathing. A person might sit on the throne and at the same time wash her hair.

Knowing full well when Sweet Cheeks was in the bathroom, I would call out from my wilted heap on the bed, "Are you in there?"

"Yes."

"How long will you be in there?"

"I dunno."

"A rough guess?"

No response.

I was content with these lazed queries when my circumstances weren't violently nagging, but I had it in me to be direct. In my repertoire was a shoulder-to-hip body block, the kind football players use, only mine was more a series of stout nudges to the tune of "Come on, come on. Get up!"

"Okay, for a minute," he would say, and then stand by as I cramped over—elbows propped on my knees, cheek bones wedged against the heels of my hands, which altogether had the effect of stretching my mouth into a hideous grin, had anyone been lying on the floor to observe. My toenails, I noticed absently, fresh out of LaCrosse Ice Pacs, weren't manicured for sandal wear.

From Oaxaca, we headed west to the beaches. But they proved too excruciatingly hot for white-bellied northerners, and cowboy tans are not strutted on the sands of Huatulco. So we pushed on to southern mountain towns. On the occasions of our all-day journeying, Baby Cakes broke down and gulped enough of the "pink gak" (Pepto-Bismol)

As soon as the bus started to sway with motion, I knew I was in trouble. I struggled internally with my dilemma. Literally. While Europe whizzed by, our guide began to berate us with more tormenting toilet tales, which only served to make my personal situation seem more urgent. I simply could not wait until the next stop.

When Mr. Hold It finished his harangue, I stood up, threw back my shoulders, walked down the aisle calmly, with my conscience clear, looking my fellow passengers squarely in the eye, and opened the little door that led to the forbidden throne. It was the flush heard round the bus!

◆

—Michelle M. Lott, "The Forbidden Throne"

---

to bind things up for the requisite eight to ten hours of jouncing on a second-class bus with no bathroom.

Then one afternoon, our bus was grinding along a dirt track up a hogback mountain and came to a spot where the ridge's width pinched down to one lane. Directly beyond, we pulled over and stopped. A small café offered an opportunity for lunch, and the disembarking passengers streamed for it. I, with other things pressing, trotted back to the narrow spot, where two outhouses stood cantilevered over the cliff. One already occupied, I sought to commandeer the other. The lower edge of a heavy, ill-fitting door was jammed against the concrete floor. I kicked and thumped and shoved. I lunged at it. Finally inside, I kicked and banged and lunged some more. Swirling apprehensions, at just how many years this structure had jutted out over thin air and just how many more minutes it might continue to do so, as well as thoughts about my contributing to the horror of what must surely be strewn down the mountainside, were completely bumped from my mind when faced with inventing new contortions to execute any business amidst the floor to ceiling filth. I gathered my long traveling skirt up around my waist and thought, *Should never have worn underwear!* One foot at a time, I gingerly stepped out of them and backed into my best bow-legged half-squat over the seatless bowl. Whew! The hard part was over. At least that's what I thought until I tried to get out. The only good leverage for opening the door, now that I could only *pull* on the knob, served to pin me in the nook created by the opened door and the seemingly never-been-flushed bowl. Someone short might have been trapped in there permanently. As it was, with one long-legged gallop, skirt clutched up in my arms, panties in hand, I emerged to sunbeams, and a queue of five fellow travelers. All eyes flew wide. I dropped my skirt. Though crimson-cheeked, I lifted my chin and affected a casual saunter toward the café. I was, I admit, uncharitably thinking: *I'm out of here! Have your own good time.* It was then that I saw the rake marks, which drew me across the hogback. Somebody's daily chore, it appeared, was to rake the dirt at cliff's edge into tidiness. I peered over and saw a dumping ground, an avalanche of human trash, from mounds of orange peels and coffee grounds to broken refrigerators and rusted car fenders. How many years' worth? I don't know. There's a metaphor here. What is it? Something to do with civilization's razorbacks and plunges—certainly not pinnacles.

To one degree or another, active bowel syndrome continued to be the order of our days. Through some act of providence, due, I'm certain, to unwarranted stretches of time served in similar straits on previous trips, I escaped the month with only a quarter of my days choreographed around various *zocalos* and their *servicios publico*. As the weeks wore on, any remnants of shithouse privacy we thought we had in this relationship vaporized.

Now any adventure, no matter how awry it goes from original plan—and particularly, it seems, if it goes far afield—provides new perspectives on, and new dimensions to, our self-aggrandized little existences on this planet. That is the inescapable residual of travel. We had ranged almost to the Guatemalan border and back, in large part overland, and I was struck by two things.

The first bolt carried an awareness of the depressingly small amount of blue sky left in the world; much of the heavens matched ocherous sandbanks. It is plainly spooky to see the sun at midday a ball of burnt-orange as though setting, directly overhead. The second flash concerned sewage, beginning with the volume I had witnessed running freely through the streets and into the sea. Beautiful warm-water bays had proved too foul for our swimming tastes. In Mexico City, which we passed through coming and going, we worked our iodine/filter system overtime on the hotel water. The sanitation problems of what is now the largest city in the world are so fierce the air's particulate matter contains fecal dust.

Surely no one's Mexican vacation has ever culminated in leaps for joy at the country's archaic methods of human waste disposal. Yet, as disheartened as I was by the sight and stench of raw sewage, I was, all told, undergoing a pleasant dawning. The problems of coping with mountains of human excrement were indeed global. In once again brushing up against this knowledge, I was delivered from the tortured days of cabin fever and returned to a state of sanity. By the time we wheeled the old truck into the unplowed snow in our home drive, my angle of focus had widened: I had assumed once more my rightful insignificance in the total scheme of things. Travel had healed me, if not in the manner I had planned.

As evidence to the degree of my cure, I was not at all fazed when the phone rang the first day we were home and a neighbor, a punctilious Epicurean accustomed to traveling in grand style, having just returned from a month in France, plunked himself smack in the middle of my subject, as though we had spoken only yesterday, and as though there were no other part to his trip. "Kathy, something goddamned disastrous happened!" In his familiar gravelly timbre from years of smoking, he related his story. "We got to Paris, a little restaurant, and I ordered *fruits de mer.* I always do, first thing." I envisioned a platter awiggle with snails, limpets, clams, mussels, winkles, langoustines, crayfish—all artfully bedded in seaweed. "Damn thing poisoned me!"

News bulletins had warned of bacterial contamination, but, unknowingly, he had downed his favorite repast. Several hours later, he was trying in a feverish attempt to mate what he called "one of those crazy French keys" with his hotel door. But alas, too late! "Went right down my pant legs, filled up my shoes," he wailed. I thought of the red velvet slipper-like shoes he had worn on Christmas and hoped those weren't the ones. If, at first, I felt a bit reluctant to share my tales of Mexico (so unsophisticated were they by comparison), shit became the almighty equalizer. Soon we were howling over journeys reduced to it and waxing philosophical with poopish travel dictums: Calculate your degree of fun by how many trips you make to the loo.

With my fresh perspective on life, I was able to see things now that previously hadn't been available to me: the existence of an annual Human Waste Conference, a national Toilet Day (in Japan), and an International Toilet Forum dedicated to celebrating and improving the world's long-neglected public restrooms. Sewage, it seemed, was undergoing a worldwide awakening. A nun in Mexico was helping residents of a mountain pueblo build a community compost toilet. In New York, eleven winning entries of an Urban Outhouse Design Competition had been on exhibit at the Municipal Art Society on Madison Avenue. In Idaho, I visited the site of a $16,000 Scat Machine, essentially a giant dishwasher for the portable toilets, JON-NY PARTNERS *et al*, coming off Salmon River rafting trips.

Not only was a whole new industry growing up around odoriferous effluvium, the stuff was entering an era of fashionability. In Italy, the artist Piero Manzoni's scatological sculptures, "*Merda d'artista*" ("Artist's Shit") were making a hit. His own excrement, which was tinned in 1961 but hadn't fetched much of a price in that decade, had begun selling for as much as $75,000 a can. In the south of France, a friend's daughter stepped out of a newfangled *pissoir,* saying, "Oh, mother, I can't believe it! Princess Stephanie was singing while I was peeing!" And the venerable poet Galway Kinnell let it be known he was writing poems about house flies and shit, trying to restore dignity to things despised.

As for me: my idea of blowing town to "get away from it all" had shown itself to be a great myth. The bungly saddles we end up carrying in life are ofttimes not to be shaken—though, I will say, they can be polished, tooled, brassed, even peacocked.

And, as I'd remembered: Travel is therapy. It can reel you back from the deep.

Kathleen Meyer is the author of the international best-selling outdoor guide How to Shit in the Woods: An Environmentally Sound Approach to a Lost Art, *with more than 1.5 million copies in print, in seven languages. Her Montana memoir,* Barefoot Hearted: A Wild Life Among Wildlife, *was published in 2001. "Toiletopia," another of her travel essays, was included in the Travelers' Tales collection* A Woman's Passion for Travel: More True Stories from A Woman's World. *Meyer makes her home with farrier Patrick McCarron in the Bitterroot Valley of western Montana. To view pictures of their covered wagon travels and draft horses, horseshoeing, barn living, orphaned bear cubs, and vistas on the Lewis and Clark Trail, visit the author at her web site:* ***www.KathleenintheWoods.com***

*

Five hours later, gas tank and bladder mandates pulled us over in a one-horse town called Coalinga, one of the few towns on Route 198, a barren highway that runs through California's Central Valley. Coalinga got its name in 1891, when the Southern Pacific Railroad laid track through the Central Valley. There were three coaling stations in the area, called A, B, and C. "Coaling A" became the town's name. But it reminded me, I told Jia-Rui, that "linga" is the word for penis in the *Kama Sutra*. Coalinga boasts two gas stations and a McDonald's, surrounded by a mystical flatland of golds and browns and not much else. McDonald's restaurants are frequently staffed by punky teenagers who don't give a shit about anything—a blessing for road-weary travelers, who can saunter freely into their bathrooms time and again without purchasing so much as a hot apple pie. After powdering our noses in the Coalinga branch, we crossed the road to refill the gas tank. Then, we consulted the map and picked our next route.

Great. O.K., let's go...ahem. *Let's go.*

The car would not start. I could not turn the key in the ignition. A light indicting "there's a problem" flashed helpfully on the dashboard. I looked at Jia-Rui and then at the key. I exhaled, pulled it out, turned it over, and tried again—still no luck. I put my head on the steering wheel and whimpered while Jia-Rui fussed with the key.

I did not want to be stuck in this podunk town named for a fossil-fuel dick. After a few more minutes of panic and prayer, I glanced down at the gear shift and found the cause of our very sorry-ass predicament: the car was in "Drive." *Stupid novice driver.*

I slipped it into "Park," put the key back in the ignition, and started the engine, which hummed agreeably. We rolled out of the gas station and out of Coalinga forever.

—Rachel Quinn, "Joshua Tree"

SUZANNE SCHLOSBERG

Great in the Sack

What an extra 50 pounds can add to a relationship.

My boyfriend, Alec, has come up with some pretty loopy ideas, but not long ago he topped himself: He suggested I run around Yerington, Nevada, with a 50-pound sack of chicken feed around my neck.

Let me explain.

On a recent road trip around the West, Alec and I were driving down the Extraterrestrial Highway, a barren stretch of highway in southern Nevada where UFO sightings are frequently reported. We stopped at a diner for pie, and Alec noticed a flyer on the window for an event called the Great American Sack Race. I assumed it was one of those three-legged races and dismissed the idea instantly.

But Alec, a veteran cop with instincts for the peculiar, kept reading. "You don't hop in the sack," he said. "You carry it. For five miles. You're strong—you could do this!" According to the flyer, the event dated back to 1910, when five farm-workers from Wabuska, Nevada, bet their boss, Harry Warren, that he couldn't carry a 120-pound sack of wheat into

Yerington, ten miles away. Harry won the bet and the Great American Sack Race was born. It is now held every four years in Yerington.

Alec read the rules aloud: "Sack must weigh 100 pounds for men and 50 pounds for women. Sack cannot have straps, belts, or buckles attached to it. Sack must be carried by corners with hands." The prize money was $1,000. I had to admit I was intrigued. Surely this was not the wackiest idea hatched along the Extraterrestrial Highway.

On the way home to Berkeley, I stopped at a feed store and bought sacks weighing 25 and 50 pounds. My plan was to start light and, over the course of three months, gradually build up strength and stamina; meanwhile, I'd beef up my weight-lifting routine at the gym.

At first, I carried my 25-pound sack everywhere—to the supermarket, to the post office, to Starbucks for a Frappuccino. On long walks, to take my mind off the crushing shoulder pain, I'd listen to radio shrink Dr. Laura Schlessinger berate her callers. One day a woman asked Dr. Laura whether it was a bad idea for her to date a married co-worker with three ex-wives. My first thought was, *Is this woman insane?* But as I shifted my sack to relieve the pressure on my trapezius, I realized that perhaps I was not in a position to judge.

Oddly, nobody in my neighborhood ever raised an eyebrow—as if it were perfectly normal to stroll around the East Bay carrying a sack of chicken feed while wearing a Sony Walkman. The only person who exhibited even an ounce of curiosity about my sack was my Fed Ex guy, who saw it on my doorstep and asked if I owned a parrot.

After a month, I was ready to graduate to the 50-pounder. Alas, it was too great a leap. Hunched over like Quasimodo, I shuffled along for one mile before the pain on my clavicle got so bad that I collapsed in agony on a park bench. Demoralized, I stopped training with my sack.

But I knew I still had to compete. I had paid my $100 entry fee and told several friends. I was in deep. Though I was too discouraged to continue training with the sack, I vowed to show up at the starting line.

Two months later, Alec and I loaded my 50-pounder into the car and drove to Yerington, a high-desert town of 2,800 with no stoplights, one supermarket, and a weekly newspaper that reports bowling scores. (Cheyenne Auto Body was leading the Night Owls league by 3.5 games.)

We parked on Main Street and walked into the casino for a bite to eat. That's when I started to get nervous. "Maybe I should buy some bananas to fuel up," I said, as if forty grams of carbohydrates could compensate for two months of inadequate training. But I was overcome by laziness and the smell of hot apple pie. I ordered the pie.

Later, while Alec played the slots, I went outside to register for the race. Just then, one of the male competitors emerged from a big, silver pickup truck. My jaw dropped. My eyes bulged out. He was Fabio—only blonder, taller, more tan, and more muscular. He carried his 100-pound sack like it was a feather pillow.

Only three women besides me had signed up for the race, and, while they did not look like Bulgarian shotputters, each was daunting in her own way. There was Mayleen, who had trained with a 66-pound sack. There was Meri, who was doing warm-up sprints down Main Street.

Then there was Vicki, winner of the last sack race in 1992, returning to defend her title. Vicki was a personal trainer and a marathon runner. More alarmingly, Vicki was eating GU (pronounced "goo"), a pudding-like gel that's popular among endurance athletes. GU is made of maltodextrin, sodium citrate, and calcium carbonate. I wondered if apple pie had any of those ingredients.

After we weighed our sacks, the race official announced to the crowd of 200 that it was time for the calcutta, a type of betting pool. "Nevada is a gambling state," he reminded everyone, as I stood there horrified. When the auctioneer called my name, I timidly walked out to the middle of Main Street so that the spectators could look me over. Apparently, I was a none-too-impressive sight. "Do I hear fifty dollars?" the auctioneer asked. "Fiftydollarsfiftydollarsfiftydollarsfiftydollars?" He heard nothing. This was depressing.

Meanwhile, where was Alec? Wasn't he going to put his money where his mouth was? Finally, he raised his hand and bought me for $50. (When I asked him later what took him so long, he said, "Hey, man, fifty bucks is fifty bucks.")

Then all nine of us competitors—five men and four women—gathered to hear the race official spell out the rules: We were to complete eight laps around the town. If our sacks touched the ground, we'd be disqualified.

Minutes later I heard over the loudspeaker, "Runners to the starting line!" This sent me into a panic. All along I had assumed this was a walk—I'd even spent $80 on special walking shoes. I turned to Alec: "He doesn't mean that *literally*, right? I mean, there's no way you could *run* with 50 pounds on your back, right?"

I don't know which one of us was more shocked when the gun fired and my eight fellow sack racers charged down the street in a sprint. Not only had I failed to train with the 50-pound sack, but I had not run in at least four years. Inside I was screaming, "Wait! Stop! Let's discuss this like rational adults!"

At this point, I had two choices: I could quit the race and spend the rest of my life listening to Alec complain about having thrown fifty bucks down the toilet. Or I could give it my best. Clenching the ends of my sack, I took off in a slow trot, hoping to run two miles and walk the rest.

But after a couple blocks, adrenaline took over. Suddenly, the sack didn't feel so heavy. I picked up speed. I passed Mayleen. I passed Meri. Then Vicki. I passed three of the five men. With three laps to go, I had built a one-minute lead on Vicki.

But then she started gaining on me. With a lap to go, she had cut my lead to thirty seconds. I picked up the pace. The crowd was cheering as I turned the final corner and crossed the finish line.

I was so thrilled that I forgot to take the sack off my shoulders. Several spectators came up to shake my hand. One woman hugged me. They all wondered where I was from and how I had trained. I wondered what it was like to live in a town with people that friendly.

And then, with the local sports columnist in earshot, I made perhaps the dumbest comment ever uttered by the winner of an athletic event: "I haven't won a trophy since I won the good citizenship award in fourth grade!" (Sadly, this fact made its way into the paper.)

At the awards ceremony I received my $1,000 check, alongside the men's winner, who'd beaten me by six minutes and Fabio by one minute. Alec won $240 in the calcutta. I insisted he buy dinner.

Suzanne Schlosberg is the author of Fitness for Travelers *and coauthor of* Fitness for Dummies *and* Weight Training for Dummies. *She has no intention of defending her title in the Great American Sack Race.*

SANDRA TSING LOH

The Perils of Leisure

Paradise—a place where fat is fine.

"I'M OLD, I'M FAT, I'M GOING TO TAHITI."

Gauguin thought it, Brando thought it, and last month it was my turn. True, those guys were older when it hit them. Then again, they weren't surrounded by today's new breed of Frighteningly Clever Twenty-Something Interns.

I mean, here I am going on thirty-three, logging fourteen-hour days, getting nowhere, and then I'm told by twenty-one-year-old Shien that I'm always clicking this wrong thing on Windows. Shien makes eight dollars an hour. Next, a slim, flannel-shirt- and nose-ring-wearing twenty-three-year-old named Nina leans in and corrects my spelling of "portentous." I thought it was "portentious." I don't know why.

Then they all flounce off to a West African *djimbe* concert. What is *djimbe*? Some hip KCRW thing, no doubt. Help! They are Stepford Interns, after my job. Which they can do better than me! Than I! What I *want* to tell them is: "Stop rocking the vote and start brewing my friggin' coffee! One day your arm fat, too, may fall!" Except I can't, because then Shien might modify my autoexec.bat file.

"Tahiti," I announce icily instead. "I'm going to take my vacation next week in Tahiti."

Tahiti, I've always felt, is the most offensive of the South Sea islands. It has no socially redeeming qualities. A topless little vixen of an island is Tahiti. Fiji, the Cook Islands, New Caledonia—all these seem intellectually complex by comparison. Even the Hawaiian Islands have become, well, oddly driven. These days, one is always four-wheeled to the back of Maui to see acres of aggressively tilled sugar cane. The University of Hilo has a U.S.-dominating women's volleyball team. *Manoa* is Hawaii's award-winning literary magazine. This is the new, brisk, forward-looking Hawaii, one senses, and everyone better get with it.

But Tahiti has been languishing lo these many years under the laconic hand of the French. Tahiti seems to do nothing but lie in a hammock in her teeny grass skirt, buff her nails, and snap, *"Oh, merde,"* when she splits one. And I like that. It's very 1803, very Golden Age of vacations. I suddenly want to go, "Argh! Me blarney leg!" and fall headfirst into a keg of rum. (Thus reenacting, I think, much of Tahiti's written history.) I may be totally wrong about this; these may be racist, sexist, imperialist comments. But…eat my shorts! I'm old, I'm fat, I'm going to Tahiti!

My fear was that people in Tahiti would not be old and fat enough. But when I arrive in Moorea, I cheer. Our Polynesian cab driver is unabashedly fat; she wears a lei; from the front seat protrudes the business end of a ukulele. Would my cruel friend Mel dare say to her, as he'd said to me: "Tahiti? And what size thong bikini are you going to wear? Large, medium, or the *stringer*?"

Why, I could be queen on this fertile island, I think exultantly. My cellulite would be sacred! "Sandra's thighs have swelled from a size ten to a size fourteen!" the natives would bellow to each other through conch shells. "Time for a celebration...and a feast of sweet, roasted pig!"

Tahiti has beaten even its Club Med into a kind of torpor. I always insist on Club Med. When I go on vacation, I demand to step from the plane, be handed an umbrella drink, and fall face first onto the sand. Club Med provides that, but their many activities can sometimes intrude; every other hour you have to run and hide from hairy Giancarlo, the water-ballet instructor.

> We can learn a little something from mid-life men, can't we? For example, if your breasts are starting to sag, why not grow armpit hair and do the old comb-over?
>
> —Leigh Anne Jasheway,
> *I'm Not Getting Older (I'm Getting Better At Denial)*

Mexico's Club Meds (where airfare is cheap, the water brisk) feature vigorous Seattle newlyweds in neon visors, high-fiving. By contrast, among Moorea's bungalows float bag-eyed French folk with barely the will to suck smoke from their cigarettes. They look like they've been disco dancing since 1984 and now wish to curl up in the fetal position on the sand and die.

But as the week evolves, I find myself bonding more and more with the French. You have to—just to escape the Australians. Before, I had no mental picture of Australia; now I understand it is much like a bowling alley in New Jersey, but bigger and with kangaroos. At our first dinner, a Sydney woman with huge frosted hair who is sawing her way through island-clubbed veal shrills: "The new Miss

America—she's deef! Absolutely deef! She dit'in even know she won. 'Ow she's going to 'andle all 'er duties and responsibilities, I dunno!"

At least she likes us. The next night we sit with Ted, a DJ from Auckland, New Zealand. He is not at all intrigued by me and my boyfriend when we're introduced, respectively, as a writer and jazz musician from L.A.

"I say, any other Kiwis here?" Ted asks distractedly, neck craning about like a gazelle's. A DJ from Phoenix, Arizona finally sparks his interest; they exchange business cards and network loudly.

By Thursday, conversation is meaningless anyway. Moorea is amazing, but after a lot of rum all tropical islands start to look alike: Vietnam in *Apocalypse Now*. The lone movie showing on our forty-seven-mile-perimeter paradise: *Beethoven's 2nd*, in French. Even the chefs go stir-crazy, making salmon in vanilla sauce with island beets and Chinese-style tortellini.

There is nothing to do, finally, but be fat. Rubenesque matrons drop their tops, the "Ooh" plopping out of their "la la's." Sixty-four-year-old Dutch businessmen drift by in *pareos,* bellies bared, hibiscus behind each ear. Then there is leathery Wayne from Vancouver—Dennis Hopper in an ACAPULCO! visor. How long has Wayne been on vacation? "A year," he murmurs through chapped lips. A year? "Certain mistakes" had been made at home, he relates, intense bright eyes darting, so he wanted to "get away from it all." Three months have been spent wandering in Costa Rica, "for the tranquility and the animals." Now it's on to Australia. Why? Leaning forward, he whispers: "Because I want to hold…a koala bear."

Koala bears everywhere will want to run for their lives; on

the other hand, Wayne is carrying Visa and American Express. And if you have those, your paradise usually will find you.

Sandra Tsing Loh writes a column for Buzz *magazine and is a commentator on National Public Radio. As a solo performer, she has been featured in the HBO* New Writers Project *and at the U.S. Comedy Festival in Aspen. She has won a Pushcart Award, and her writing has appeared in* Glamour, Elle, Harper's Bazaar, *and* Cosmopolitan. *This story was excerpted from her book,* Depth Takes a Holiday: Essays from Lesser Los Angeles. *She lives in Van Nuys, California.*

*

I am fat. I have a belly that wobbles when I walk and a bum that echoes my movements. Don't get me wrong. This is not some life-changing confession à la Alcoholics Anonymous: "Hello, my name is Lara and I am fat." Rather, it's an easy way for you to picture me, climbing up a rope, ass over end into the back of a rocking Indonesian fishing boat, desperately trying not to bounce into the propeller and to retain, well, at least a crumb of dignity.

Backpacking is always adventurous, but it takes on many new twists when a plus-size body meets rickety transport, bamboo bridges, and tiny locals who find all Westerners—let alone those with wobbly bellies—startling.

—Lara McKinley, "Backpacking with a Belly in Indonesia"

NANCY BARTLETT

Panic, In Any Other Language

A mother tries her best to maintain grace and dignity when caught in a compromising position.

ONE SUMMER, IN A FIT OF INSANITY, MY PARTNER AND I held our two sets of teenagers captive in a minivan for a three-week tour of Europe. Incessant moaning about being separated from girlfriends and boyfriends began well before the plane touched down, and as soon as we drove away from the Europcar office the kids went for each other's throats.

Tensions relaxed a bit as the damp forests and green pastures of the Austrian Alps fell behind, and we were all distracted by the dry lushness of Italy's grains and grapes. Driving through the Dolomites the kids saw ruined villas and friar's cells on every rocky prominence as if their tenth-grade World History classes had suddenly sprung to life.

The surroundings affected my partner and me a little differently. High on the adventure of the first touch of the heated south, and having left all that Lutheran influence behind, we began thinking *amoré*. The kids, in back with the map, argued knowledgeably about what had happened to whom, when and where in this land that figured so large in their textbooks, and quoted Shakespeare. Up front, like hormone-driven adolescents, my boyfriend and I whispered of stolen moments in the shadow of ruins and of what we would do in secret while the kids were busy taking pictures of one another beside fountains. By the time we arrived in Verona, the temperature had risen to such a point that I changed into a black minidress and, naughtily, left my underwear in the car.

As a simpatico family group we walked the town, gawked at crumbling buildings and tried our first Italian words on money-changers and merchants. Inspired by a setting famed for secret love, T and I sneaked kisses while the kids inspected architecture. Finally, sharing *gelato* in six newly acquired flavors—*mandarine, fragola, melone, pesca, strachiatella,* and the hands down favorite, mango—we sauntered to our actual destination: Juliet's house.

The garden wasn't quite as lush as the Zefferelli movie version and we scoffed at the idea of a teenage boy, no matter how smitten, scaling the sheer twenty-foot walls, but we gave in to poetic license and the romantic thrall of legend. Later, with all our goals for the city accomplished, we began the long walk back to the car. Following the shortest route—according to the map provided by the *ufficio touristico*—we found ourselves winding through town along the Veronese version of Rodeo Drive. We passed Prada, La Perla, Max Mara, and Armani stores with windows full of beguiling merchandise. Dressed in travel casual and sweaty from our drive, we lusted, but didn't venture inside. We'd almost cleared the shopping district when a swimwear boutique whose window proclaimed *Vendita!* caught my eye. From the size of the crowd and the price-tag shape of the many signs, I deduced that this was a sale. A swimsuit was on my short list of items to buy in Italy so, though time was tight, I decided to check out the event. My boyfriend let himself be persuaded quickly enough, and after a little grumbling the kids agreed to find other shops to explore while I tried on suits. They gave me twenty minutes.

Decorated in opulent Eurostyle, the boutique featured polished white marble floors, gilded mirrors, and Etruscan-influenced drapery rods. Urns of blazing flowers stood on display tables. An expansive antique desk served as sales counter.

Threading my way through the crowd of chic Italian women, I figured out the layout and found the rack for my size. Given a clientele dressed in tailored summer-weight suits, their hair swept into perfect up-dos, I suspected that when I tried to convert the thousands of lira into dollars, even the shop's sale prices would prove too high. But how could I pass up the opportunity to do math in an elegant private fitting room while wearing a designer bikini?

After picking out a few I liked, I glanced around to locate the fitting room. Something touched my ankle. I looked down. A bright red circle gleamed at me from the polished white marble between my black sandals. "How odd," I thought, "it looks as if someone has shot the floor. It's bleeding." The truth took a moment to register: my tampon was leaking.

I slapped my foot over the drop and, cheeks burning, took stock. I was standing in the middle of a swanky boutique, surrounded by coifed women I could not speak to, hands full of expensive garments, with blood ready to run down my legs all over the white floor. I had no underwear on, no way to shift my clothing to stop the flow. Oh, I was too sexy.

There was no time to reflect upon my folly, or on which

mischievous god was so bent on exposing my hypocrisies. Clamping my legs together I scooted sideways between two rapidly chatting women, shoved the suits onto the nearest rack then carefully sidled over to the tall, elegant blonde at the cash register. I had no idea what to say. The first word that came to mind was *prego*, which didn't sound right. She would hear nothing but an out-of-context plea, while I would be stuck searching for the next word and confused about spaghetti sauce. I managed *"scuzi"* then just stammered: "uh paper, uh *papier*, uh *serviette*, uh *acqua*," resorting at last to a pantomime of handwashing. She stared at me blankly, then seemed to get my drift and moved to the rear of the shop, pointed past a wall and said something. I thanked her and, without moving my legs too far apart, went in the direction she pointed. As I passed, she glanced down. I played up the limp, hoping she thought I had a bad leg.

Watching the tiles of the hallway behind me for any telltale red drops, I slowly made my way to the back room where I found a toilet, a sink and a few cleaning supplies. I sat in a hurry and relaxed, thankful the episode hadn't been any more mortifying.

I washed, then reached into the change pocket of my travel pouch for another tampon. I checked the large pocket where I keep my passport. I looked in the long zippered compartment that holds my bills. I searched through every zippered pocket and Velcro compartment twice. Then I searched them all again. I plunged my hands into the patch pockets of my dress and found a used roll of film. And then I remembered; I'd been unconcerned about bringing an extra because we were only going to be in Verona for an hour. I cursed and I swore. Poison seemed like a good idea.

I never steal, but now was the time to start. Desperate,

I ransacked the cupboards. Nothing. Stunned, I sat there wondering what to do. Finally, having no other ideas, I rolled up a wad of toilet paper and pressed it into the site. With a deep breath, I moved out into the hall again taking tiny steps.

Pretending to be shopping proved to be good camouflage, but once I'd made a circuit of the shop I faced the door like an agoraphobic, knowing that outside I'd have to stride out a little more. On the street, I had no idea which way to go. I looked up and down for family members then checked my watch. It was past time to meet in the square. They would sit waiting for me for ten minutes or so before losing their tempers and beginning to bicker again. The paper would be soaked by then. I couldn't stand here until help came. And I knew no shop on Rodeo Drive sold feminine products, so going back the two blocks would be useless. I inched toward the corner moving my legs only from the knee down thinking I must look like Jack Lemmon mincing around in drag in *Some Like it Hot*.

Halfway up the next block I spotted a sign—*Farmacia*. Now that word I'd picked up from the guidebook since it was closely allied to the warning about drinking only bottled water. With my cartoon gait, I scuttled off toward the shop. Surely they'd have tampons, and if not, I could get my poison there.

I opened the heavy wood and glass door to find another hurdle. The shop was an old-fashioned pharmacy where you have to ask for what you want and the clerk digs it out from behind the counter or the back room. The jangling bell brought the cheerful shopkeeper saying, "*Buon giorno*." I smiled brightly but silently groaned. We'd already learned that in Europe items aren't grouped the way they are in the U.S. We'd visited tobacco shops to find phone cards, and in

Amsterdam had been thrown out of a coffee shop for daring to bring the kids in, and later learned they really sell a smokier substance. Maybe tampons weren't sold in Italian pharmacies. Where would they be found? What would they be called? What would the package look like? I hadn't noticed any vending machines in *toiletten* in Germany. Did tampons even exist in Italy? I might be facing a whole new adventure here. I mentally kicked myself for not studying that section of the guidebook. With nothing to do but take a stab at communication, I shuffled up to the smiling clerk and stammered again.

It's amazing how effective stammering can be. I don't know what I actually said. I just threw out words modified to sound vaguely Italian. *Tampon, feminina, serviette* again, *luna.* I accompanied my words with sign language meant to depict a small cylinder with a dangling string. Italians speak with their hands, so that's probably what did it. Somehow the woman understood me and *voilà,* from a low shelf behind her, produced the wanted item and held it out to me, a question in her voice. I nodded, *"Si, Si!"*

We got through the lire part reasonably smoothly and I said *"Grazie, grazie!"* over and over as I backed out into the street wondering "what next?" On the stoop, I cast around for alternatives. I couldn't face going back to the boutique and asking to use the *acqua* again. I didn't remember what a public restroom was called. The kids had the map. I had to risk the bar across the street.

Having read of, but not yet experienced, the various ways continental establishments charge for refreshment served standing, sitting, inside, outside, with service, without service, I was a little worried about the protocol and cost of sitting in the place I required. But there was nothing else to do. I decided to be bold and tottered into the bar as if I owned it, then made my way straight to the most logical site for a restroom. In the *signoras*, I made my switch with relief and relaxed clenched muscles.

Unwilling to appear an ugly American, I took an extra few moments to stop at the counter and buy a bottle of *acqua*, one of the few things I knew I could ask for with the right word. I cheerfully laid out all the lire the barman could want. He flirted a little as he took the right number and I laughed as if I understood. He might have been making rude comments about how idiotic I'd looked when I came in, but now I didn't care. A strategically placed wad of cotton can have an amazing effect on your self-confidence.

I swung out into the sun again, turned the corner and ran smack into my two feuding families. Allied for once, they fumed at me for keeping them waiting, for scaring them to death with my disappearance and, finally, for making us late.

Faced with all this anger, I laughed at the comedy of the whole afternoon, which only made them madder. I said, "Hey, I am woman. I can deal effectively with some fascinating situations. And if you will kindly cease this strife, I'll tell you the whole, tragic story."

Nancy Bartlett has been a reporter, technical writer, and construction project manager, and is currently adventuring in the wilds of software development. Her essays on family, nature, and life have appeared in Northwest newspapers and in Brain, Child *magazine. She lives with her family on Whidbey Island in Washington State where she is publicist for the Whidbey Island Writers' Conference.*

*

"I want to spend more time with you. Why don't you stay with me in Monterosso?"

I looked at Claudio in his white Dolce and Gabbana tank top, Speedo thong, and filled-to-the-brim fanny pack. I plan my spontaneity and I look before I leap. In other words, I roll with the flow like a cinder block. I started to decline, "You've NO idea how tempted I am...I mean you really don't. But I can't. I'd like to, but it won't work out. I need to work on this article and..." but he cut me off with a hug—warm, strong, melting—and a kiss—soft, lingering, teasing. I watched my caution carried out with the *Mezzorgiorno* and agreed to meet him later that night at the La Spezia train station.

I raced back to the hotel, and figured with a shower and the bus ride I'd get to the bus station at 9:00 P.M., our pre-arranged meeting time. I unpacked my gauzy flowered dress, which whispered with promise, and got into the shower, soaping myself for a night of romance and fantasy. Mid-loofah I made a discovery that probably thousands of woman all over the world were making at that moment—some with tears of relief, others with indifference, and many like myself with Munch-scream expressions, "No! This is not happening! I cannot be getting my period right now!!"

—Heather Bloch, "In Quest of Plus Value"

JENNIFER L. LEO

A Prude in Patpong

A bashful traveler finds liberation in the realm of the bird woman.

I HAD HEARD ABOUT BANGKOK'S INFAMOUS RED LIGHT district many times. Mostly I had heard about the in-your-face sex offerings, and imagined sleazy men who couldn't get laid at home coming here for the easy and exotic. I pictured doorway after doorway stationed with fourteen-year-old girls in short skirts and too much makeup.

I also had been told that women weren't the only things being sold. Men and animals would be readily available too. I wondered if a nice underused thirty-something male was on the menu and a friend didn't hesitate in saying that it was certainly possible...that anything was possible in Patpong.

I wasn't sure that I wanted to see *all* that was possible in Patpong. R-rated sex scenes in movies sometimes made me blush and I certainly wasn't the type who enjoyed watching porn. At the same time, I knew that there was no way I was going to miss out on the hooker headquarters of the world. I was traveling with my friend Susan, a California soccer mom of three with an agenda to be comfortable. I seriously doubted that she had any desire to go there with me, so it would have to wait until after she left. Or would it?

On our last evening at The Oriental hotel, Susan and I hooked up with two Americans and a Scotsman, Rolf, Tom, and Jim. In the Bamboo Bar we swapped stories about our travels. One round of drinks led to a second and it was only natural that Jim's "Slippery Nipple" led to Rolf's recount of his Tantric sex class, and then on to a suggested field trip to Patpong. Why wouldn't it? When the boys had heard that we were Patpong virgins, they felt it was their responsibility as gentlemen to escort us to this not-to-be-missed Bangkok highlight. But who was really escorting whom?

When our cab dropped us off, I looked up to see a big green sign over the length of the street as if we had just reached Main Street USA at Disneyland. But where were the naked women? All I could see was a street crowded with tables of souvenirs. It looked like a night market, not the be-all end-all of sex streets.

I paused a moment to take off my long-sleeved sweater. Beneath it I was wearing a black strappy top that was more appropriate for the steamy humidity of Bangkok's streets, even after midnight. Rolf raised his arms and started to dance in front of me as if we were going to start our own show.

More than one friend, on more than one occasion, had suggested that I could find "temp work" on Patpong if I were to run out of money. The fact that I spoke English would allow me to command a higher price. Hmmm...by Rolf's reaction, maybe they were right. I wondered if I could up the price for my soft jiggling belly as well.

We walked down the center aisle. Easily distracted by Thai silk purses, wooden placemats, and silver jewelry I momentarily forgot why we were there.

"Ping-pong show! Ping-pong show!" called a young Thai tout vying for our attention, but mostly our business.

"Ping pongs are so old," said Rolf, ending the shopping crawl and leading us down the side of the street where we could see the sex bars.

I tentatively peeked in one of the doorways and saw about a half dozen Asian women standing on a stage. Another six to eight women stood below them…altogether a double-decker treatment of Frederick's of Hollywood lingerie models. Or not, half the women were topless.

I looked the other way, not wanting to stare. Ahead, Rolf and Susan were perusing a menu board. As I peered over their shoulders, I found that they were not looking at tropical drink options, but rather a show list to what was going on inside the bar in front of us. All I could see on the mounted sheet was pussy, pussy, pussy and many different non-human things this revered female body part could perform with.

Focus returned when I saw the word "fish" three-quarters of the way down the page. I stopped reading when I saw the word "bird." No way, a bird? Could they mean a live bird? What kind of bird could allow itself to be stuffed inside a woman and then trained to fly out? What kind of double-jointed avian creature…a canary? A finch? There's no way these tiny Thai women—I don't care how many years of Kegel exercise they've done—could fit a pigeon, let alone a seagull into their honey pot. I looked around, wheels spinning hard, had I seen or even heard any birds since I arrived in Bangkok?

"A bird?" was all I could say. Rolf was negotiating with the doorman. One hundred baht each for a beer and the shows.

"No way, a bird?" I was dumbfounded. Rolf said that Susan and I should wait outside while he and Jim went up to make sure the price didn't triple once we were inside.

"I've got to see the bird show," is all I could utter back. We weren't listening to him and followed the boys up the stairs into the black room. The bird woman was somewhere inside and if I could last through all the other shows, I'd get to see her...meet her...and shake her hand. Well, I think I'd skip that last one, with all due respect.

All the walls were black and the stage was empty. A fluorescent sign on the wall opposite ours said NO PICTURE TAKING. Maybe that's because after the bird show, a camera was going to drop out of the next woman and take a Polaroid of us surrounded by smooth Thai flesh.

We were the only ones in the audience except for an Asian man engulfed by four smiling girls. One on each side, one rubbing his back, and another one just standing there ready to sub in at any moment.

A couple of naked girls got on stage and started to dance to Thai club music. Or at least that's what I thought they were doing. They mostly hung out on the sides of the stage where the poles were, and bounced. Sort of. If that's what you call it when you don't have the upfront equipment to constitute any kind of up and down movement normally associated with bouncing.

So, what was this? It wasn't a strip tease since they were already naked. It couldn't be sexy since they were twig thin and didn't have a voluptuous curve on their bodies. And their dance moves would make any white man with two left feet look like a hall-of-famer from *Solid Gold*. I must say, I was disappointed.

"Why are they so apathetic?" I asked no one in particular. I just couldn't imagine the guys I knew being turned on by this. One of the boys mumbled back a response, eyes glued to the stage.

I could be more seductive than this doing a strip tease on one leg, even with my body that only got made fun of in high school.

Then a girl came around and handed out long, tall, phallic-shaped, colored balloons. I took one and figured we'd wave it like a #1 sign whenever we saw something we liked. I'd save mine for the bird woman.

Obviously, I hadn't read the menu. The girls on stage were suddenly accessorized with a six- to eight-inch pipe that they placed in their you-know-what to use as a cannon for launching darts. Before I could look from one girl to the next, darts were flying off the stage and popping balloons hung up around them!

Realizing what was happening, I looked down at the green balloon in my hand, and then immediately at Rolf, our Patpong veteran. He was holding his balloon over his head. A girl on stage got into position to fire.

"Aaah!" I thrust my balloon into Rolf's free hand and jumped as quickly as I could to the other side of the room. What if they missed? Dart in the eyeball? No thanks. But the truth was, I just didn't want the frontal view of some strange woman's private parts, let alone to look down a pipe and into her birth canal.

Good thing too, because her first dart didn't have enough "oomph" to pop Rolf's first balloon. However, that must've just been a warm-up. From my view on the side, darts were whizzing toward my table with good speed. Susan got points from me for staying in her seat next to Jim, even if she didn't take a balloon.

When all the balloons were popped, I came back to my chair in time for the basket passing. We threw in 20 baht and 100 baht notes. I have to admit, I was impressed. I don't think I could throw a dart across the room with that kind of accuracy.

I stayed to watch show after show, open-eyed, while girls in their twenties took turns performing the unthinkable: drawing pictures of fisherman with an inserted marker, opening non-twist-off capped bottles of water, extracting three feet of glow-in-the-dark plastic flower ropes that they draped around themselves or flung around to add some action to their dancing.

It was only when they brought out the razors that I turned away and nursed my beer. I refused to look, there was no way I was going to support that. Yes, a woman was actually extracting a dozen razors on a string from her vagina. I turned around at the end when she took the razors and made a number of quick slices through a piece of

---

Eight thousand miles from suburbia, I sat in a Bangkok nightclub that featured "live nude entertainment." After downing a few drinks to make the antics on stage tolerable, I found myself goading my traveling companion to join the dancers. I even offered her money. She refused, until an artist began painting dancers with day-glo paint. Another drink, a wad of baht, and she agreed. We begged, cajoled, and finally bribed the artist to paint one more body. Fifteen minutes later she emerged, proudly showing off her fluorescent breasts to all. I took several pictures, but when I returned home I found that no one would print them. To this day, those day-glo boobs remain trapped on celluloid, unable to escape.

◆

—Susan Brady, "A Taste of the Night"

---

paper. I was horrified. If she could do this, a bird seemed manageable. A fish? A piece of cake.

I couldn't take it all in. The women and the music entranced me. I didn't realize I was grooving until one of the girls came up and asked me to get up and dance.

"Thai dancing, Thai dancing!" she said to me with outstretched hands. There was no way I was getting up there. If I stood up to dance with her, it'd be about two seconds before they had me on stage with Ms. Tweety Bird.

"No, no," I said mustering every bit of bashfulness in my body and trying to keep the rest of me from moving to the music. It was kind of hard to stay still, a part of me wanted to show these girls how to dance just a tiny bit better. Gyrations 101.

The girl left me alone and when I turned around another was telling Susan about her kids, and another was kneeling beside Rolf.

"Jennifer, did you just grab my leg?" Rolf asked smiling and sneaking his right arm into a protective position across his lap.

"What?" How could I talk to Rolf at a time like this, three women on stage were starting to light cigarettes.

"Jennifer, stop grabbing my leg," Rolf said. "This girl here is telling me that was you who just touched my leg."

All I could do was raise both of my hands to prove I was at least three feet away from his leg. My eyes couldn't leave the three women lying down on the stage and inserting lit cigarettes into their hoo-has. What would the Cancer Society say about this? I wondered if the girls were getting a buzz.

"She's my fiancée," Rolf explained quite calmly to the giggling girl trying to get into his lap, "aren't you, Jennifer?

"We're getting married," he continued. The "M" word

perked me up. I looked at him, then at her, and nodded. He needed my help. I looked at my naked ring finger and put it in my lap before he said, "Yes, really. August 16th." Two smiling Thai girls came over to shake my hand and congratulate me.

I stopped to think about this. There were decent thirty-year-old men available in Patpong! I was in the middle of a very new and ingenious way to go about husband hunting. Going to grad school had always been my fall-back plan for getting my M.R.S. degree, but escorting studly adventurous hunks to sex clubs in Bangkok could be much quicker and cost effective. After all, how many men have the courage to ask AND set a date?

But even a fun, handsome man mentioning the "M" word couldn't distract me from what was on stage. The girls weren't just having a puff on these cigarettes, they were toking away! Half way through the cig, and generating some serious ash, smoke was steadily rising above them in bursting puffs. I couldn't believe what I was seeing. They smoked the cigarette all the way down without one flinch from a single singe in the pubic region.

Susan leaned over to me and said she was ready to go. She could smell a stench that I wasn't picking up.

"What about the bird woman?" I asked. Rolf asked one of the girls before we agreed to leave.

"She's got a headache tonight. No bird," replied the girl.

The fish girl had the same story. Or was it the same woman? I didn't know or care. Heck, I didn't want to leave. Where was that menu card? What stunt would they substitute for the femme finch-tale?

While I scanned the room for feathers and fins, I looked for my good girl badge, too. The next act on stage was a woman blowing out a fake birthday cake with at least ten candles on it. I laughed in utter amazement as I hurried to catch up with my friends. This adventure deserved a song to go with it. "I Left My Blush in Bangkok," now that's a tune you can gyrate to.

Jennifer L. Leo has no permanent address but can be seen entering movie theaters in Oregon, California, and Australia. She is the creator of WrittenRoad.com, a member of Wild Writing Women, and the editor of this book.

*

As I sat down, my mother cocked an eyebrow at me. It seemed to say, "Will you do it? Even with these Americans right here?"

Her skepticism was well placed. As I unhooked my sundress, I schooled my face and manner, despite a rising blush in my cheeks, with a calculated nonchalance. Inside, my modesty was shrieking at me to leave my bathing suit top on. I reasoned that like I, they too might be here in Greece to indulge in a decidedly European liberalism. Like a mantra, I repeated *when in Rome, when in Rome* to myself as I pulled the top awkwardly over my head.

Full of myself, I sat up to casually wipe off a small pile of sand on my towel down by my feet.

Before I knew what had happened, the beach chair snapped shut like a Venus flytrap capturing its prey. I let out a small whoop of surprise as my ankles sandwiched against my head. As I struggled to right myself, I tangled in the wires of the headphones. My book was squashed in the fold of my belly and my arms were flailing, trying to grab hold of something stable. All the while, my breasts were flopping around most gracelessly, jostling against book and towel and chair. And my mother was cackling, loudly and hysterically, making no move whatsoever to help me as she wiped tears from her eyes. Out of the corner of my eye, I could see the astonished looks of the two American couples.

—Loren Drummond, "On the Way to Shameless"

CHRISTIE ECKARDT

Panties or Prison

It's all in the way you walk.

DRYDEN IN *LAWRENCE OF ARABIA* DESCRIBED THE deserts of the Arabian Peninsula as "a burning, fiery furnace," and for good reason. Summer temperatures can reach up to 140 degrees Fahrenheit. You go through several sets of clothes on any given day and today is no exception.

Since I haven't had a chance to do laundry in a few days, I am stuck with a baggy but well-ventilated pair of underwear. Wearing a long skirt I set out for the local grocery store on the other side of a six-lane street. I reach the intersection and notice that my underwear is not feeling exactly the way it should. Standing next to all these stopped cars, I can't exactly hike it up. I'm in a Muslim country. Muslims prefer not to see a woman's calf or forearm, much less watch her adjusting her skivvies. I need to find a private spot.

The parking lot is buzzing and someone is sitting inside every parked car to keep the air conditioning running. Inside the store, I am starting to get nervous so I look for an empty aisle where I can make my vertical adjustment. My underwear is now flying at half-mast. I am convinced that the cold air in the freezer aisle has shrunken my gluteus maximus as the "traitor" makes its way toward the floor posthaste. Where did all these people come from? Don't you have homes to go to? Preferably now?

I decide it's best to go home. I quickly buy a bag of groceries but by the time I get to the door the "sail" is way below half-mast, maintaining position due to an interesting walking style allowing my upper legs to hold them in place. This is funny in a desperate kind of way. Two minutes later when I arrive at the intersection I find my panties wedged between my knees. The pedestrian light is turning green. I have to walk across three lanes of stopped traffic with the real chance that my underwear may fall onto the street. This isn't so funny after all. I start to panic.

What will I do if they fall? Stop and pick them up? Just step out of them and walk on as if they aren't mine? When was the last time you saw underwear fall from the heavens? I can just hear some guy say, "Hey you're the girl whose underwear fell off on 11th Street, aren't you!" That is if I don't get thrown into prison for indecency. If I do go to prison, maybe I can shave my head and pose as a man until I can book a flight to Siberia. My head is spinning.

I decide I will just walk out of them and not go home until the traffic is long gone so no one knows where I live. But I don't. People are staring at me for the way I am hobbling across the street. They are feeling sorry for me for whatever walking disability I have. I start to laugh, imagining what I must look like to them and I have to stop in the middle of the street as my gravity-loving underwear now travel to my calves. I am imagining my inevitable cellmate. Oh, why didn't I wear pants? Who invented underwear anyway? Can you declare a jihad on the elastic industry? I manage to make it across the street after the light turns green. Nobody even honks at me to get out of the way, probably feeling sorry for me, being maimed and all. My legs are cramping from clenching to hold the underwear up.

But it doesn't end there. A group of Pakistani men are sitting on the grassy area between the corner and my door, so I have to make it past them. Walking the length of a single house takes me eight minutes. Finally, as I approach my door, my bag of groceries slips out of my grasp and spills its contents onto the sidewalk. Without thinking, I crouch down to get them. BOOM! My skivvies hit the pavement. I can't get up without them showing around my ankles. Of course at that moment a man on a bicycle comes up behind me kindly waiting for me to move aside so he can pass. Catch-22.

After giggling, half-crying, and mumbling something like "Please just go around," I manage to half-hop and drag myself out of the way as if my knees are surgically attached to my breastbone and my ankles fused to my posterior. I fall into the terrace safe from the public eye. Tears of relief and amusement spill through uncontrollable laughter. Inside, I throw away all similarly stretched underwear lurking in the back of my drawer. I make a mental note to rewrite guidebooks to this region. Tight undies are a must!

Christie Eckardt is a web site designer and children's muralist with an affection for the unknown. The portability of her "career" has allowed her to raft Nepal's coldest rivers, nearly be trampled in a raid in Bangkok's red-light district, and bring in Y2K on the shores of Vietnam. She currently divides her time between Germany and the United Arab Emirates.

SARAH VOWELL

Take the Cannoli

All obsessions lead to Italy.

THERE COMES A TIME HALFWAY THROUGH ANY HALFWAY decent liberal arts major's college career when she no longer has any idea what she believes. She flies violently through air polluted by conflicting ideas and theories, never stopping at one system of thought long enough to feel at home. All those books, all that talk, and, oh, the self-reflection. Am I an existentialist? A Taoist? A transcendentalist? A modernist, a postmodernist? A relativist-positivist-historicist-dadaist-deconstructionist? Was I Apollonian? Was I Dionysian (or just drunk)? Which was right and which was wrong, *im*pressionism or *ex*pressionism? And while we're at it, is there such a thing as right and wrong?

Until I figured out that the flight between questions is itself a workable system, I craved answers, rules. A code. So by my junior year, I was spending part of every week, sometimes every day, watching *The Godfather* on videotape.

The Godfather was an addiction. And like all self-respecting addicts, I did not want anyone to find out about my habit.

Which was difficult considering that I shared a house with my boyfriend and two other roommates, all of whom probably thought my profound interest in their class schedules had to do with love and friendship. But I needed to know when the house would be empty so I could watch snippets of the film. Sometimes it took weeks to get through the whole thing. If I had a free hour between earth science lab and my work-study job, I'd sneak home and get through the scene where Sonny Corleone is gunned down at the toll booth, his shirt polka-dotted with bullet holes. Or, if I finished writing a paper analyzing American mediocrity according to Alexis de Tocqueville, I'd reward myself with a few minutes of Michael Corleone doing an excellent job of firing a pistol into a police captain's face. But if the phone rang while I was watching, I turned off the sound so that the caller wouldn't guess what I was up to. I thought that if anyone knew how much time I was spending with the Corleones, they would think it was some desperate cry for help. I always pictured the moment I was found out as a scene from a movie, a movie considerably less epic than *The Godfather.* My concerned boyfriend would eject the tape from the VCR with a flourish and flush it down the toilet like so much cocaine. Then my parents would ship me off to some treatment center where I'd be put in group therapy with a bunch of Trekkies.

I would sit on my couch with the blinds drawn, stare at the TV screen, and imagine myself inside it. I wanted to cower in the dark brown rooms of Don Corleone, kiss his hand on his daughter's wedding day, explain what my troubles were, and let him tell me he'll make everything all right. Of course, I was prepared to accept this gift knowing that someday—and that day may never come—I may be called upon to do a service. But, he would tell me, "Until that day, accept this justice as a gift on my daughter's wedding day."

"*Grazie*, Godfather." It was as simple as that.

Looking back, I wonder why a gangster movie kidnapped my life. *The Godfather* had nothing to do with me. I was a feminist, not Italian, and I went to school at Montana State. I had never set foot in New York, thought ravioli came only in a can, and wasn't blind to the fact that all the women in the film were either virgins, mothers, whores, or Diane Keaton.

I fell for those made-up, sexist, East Coast thugs anyway. Partly it was the clothes; fashionwise, there is nothing less glamorous than snow-blown, backpacking college life in the Rocky Mountain states. But the thing that really attracted me to the film was that it offered a three-hour peep into a world with clear and definable moral guidelines; where you know where you stand and you know who you love; where honor was everything; and the greatest sin wasn't murder but betrayal.

My favorite scene in the film takes place on a deserted highway with the Statue of Liberty off in the distance. The don's henchman Clemenza is on the road with two of his men. He's under orders that only one of them is supposed to make the ride back. Clemenza tells the driver to pull over. "I gotta take a leak," he says. As Clemenza empties his bladder, the man in the backseat empties his gun into the driver's skull. There are three shots. The grisly, back-of-the-head murder of a rat-fink associate is all in a day's work. But Clemenza's overriding responsibility is to his family. He takes a moment out of his routine madness to remember that he had promised his wife he would bring dessert home. His instruction to his partner in crime is an entire moral manifesto in six little words: "Leave the gun. Take the cannoli."

I loved Clemenza's command because of its total lack of ambiguity. I yearned for certainty. I'd been born into rock-solid Christianity, and every year that went by, my faith eroded a little more, so that by the time I got to college I was a recent, and therefore shaky, atheist. Like a lot of once devout people who have lost religion, I had holes the size of heaven and hell in my head and my heart. Once, I had had a god, commandments, the promise of redemption, and a bible, The Bible, which offered an explanation of everything from creation on through to the end of the world. I had slowly but surely replaced the old-fashioned exclamation points of hallelujahs with the question marks of modern life. God was dead and I had whacked him.

Don Corleone, the Godfather, was not unlike God the father—loving and indulgent one minute, wrathful and judgmental the next. But the only "thou shalt" in the don's dogma was to honor thy family. He dances with his wife, weeps over his son's corpse, dies playing in the garden with his grandson, and preaches that "a man who doesn't spend time with his family can never be a real man."

Don Corleone would not have paid actual money to sit in fluorescent-lit rooms listening to frat boys from Spokane babble on about Descartes, boys in baseball caps whose most sacred philosophical motto could be summarized as "I drink therefore I am." Don Corleone had no time for mind games and conjecture. I, on the other hand, had nothing but time for such things, probably because I'm a frivolous female: "I spend my life trying not to be careless," the don tells his son Michael. "Women and children can be careless, but not men,"

The Godfather is a film crammed with rules for living. Don't bow down to big shots. It's good when people owe you. This drug business is dangerous. Is vengeance going to bring your son back to you or my boy to me? And then there is the grandeur, the finality, the conviction of the mantra "Never tell anybody outside the family what you're thinking again."

That last one was a rule I myself could follow. Not only did I not tell anyone outside my family what I was thinking, I was pretty tight-lipped with family too. If I was confused about the books I was reading in school, I was equally tormented by my seemingly tranquil life. At twenty-one, I was squandering my youth on hard work and contentment. I had two jobs, got straight A's. I lived with my boyfriend of three years, a perfectly nice person. We were well-suited to the point of boredom, enjoying the same movies, the same music, the same friends. We didn't argue, which meant we didn't flirt. I'd always dreamed of *The Taming of the Shrew* and I was living in—well, they don't write dramas about young girls who settle for the adventure that is mutual respect, unless you count *thirtysomething*, and I already had the same haircut as the wifely actress who smiled politely waiting for her husband to come home to their comfortable house. Thanks largely to the boyfriend's decency and patience, my parents and I were getting along better than ever. My sister was my best friend. We all lived within ten blocks of each other, one big happy family, frequently convening for get-togethers and meals. Friends clamored for dinner invitations to my parents' home, acquaintances told the boyfriend and me that we renewed their faith in love, and every time I turned in an essay exam my professors' eyes lit up. I was a good daughter, a good sister, a good girlfriend, a good student, a good citizen, a responsible employee. I was also antsy, resentful, overworked, and hemmed in.

Just as I did not divulge my secret rendezvous with *The Godfather*, I didn't talk about my claustrophobia. I didn't tell anyone that maybe I didn't want to be known only as my sister's sister or my parents' daughter or my boyfriend's girlfriend, that maybe I'd lived in that town too long and I wanted to go someplace where I could leave the house for ten minutes without running into my seventh-grade math teacher. So I told them all I wanted to study abroad to better my chances of getting into graduate school, which sounds a lot better than telling the people who love you that you'd love to get away from them.

I have a few weeks after Christmas before I have to report to Holland for a semester of art history. I fly to Vienna. I get on a train there and another one in Berlin, and another after that, and one thing leads to another and I find myself in Italy. How did that happen? Oh well, as long as I'm in Florence, perhaps I should pop down and give Sicily a look-see.

The fact is, my little freedom flight isn't working out as well as I'd hoped. I swing between the giddiness of my newfound solitude and the loneliness of same. I make a lot of panicked phone calls to my boyfriend from museums that begin with descriptions of Brueghel paintings and end with my sobbing. "What am I going to do?" I am homesick, and since I can't go home, I might as well go to the next closest thing—Sicily. I *know* Sicily. And I love the part of *The Godfather* when Michael's hiding out, traipsing around his ancestral hills, walking the streets of his father's birthplace, Corleone.

I take a night train from Rome down the boot and wake up in the Sicilian capital, Palermo. I feel ridiculous. I thought of myself as a serious person and it didn't seem like serious people travel hundreds of miles out of their way to walk in the footsteps of Al Pacino.

I don't feel so silly, however, that I'm above tracking down a bakery and buying a cannoli, my first. I walk down to the sea and eat it. It's sweeter than I thought it would be, more dense. The filling is flecked with chocolate and candied orange. Clemenza was right: Leave that gun! Take that cannoli!

> Traveling is the ruin of all happiness! There's no looking at a building here after seeing Italy.
>
> —Fanny Burney

The town of Corleone really exists and can be reached by bus. I checked. Every day I go to the travel office in Palermo to buy a ticket to the Godfather's hometown. And every morning, when I stand before the ticket agent, I can never quite bring myself to say the word "Corleone" out loud to a real live Sicilian. Because you know they know. Idiot Americans and their idiot films. I have my dignity.

So each morning when the ticket agent asks, "Where to?" one of two things happens: I say nothing and just walk off and spend the day in Palermo reading John Irving novels on a bench by the sea, or I utter the name of a proper, art-historically significant town instead. As if the clerk will hear me say, "Agrigento," and say to himself, "Oh, she's going to see the Doric temple. Impressive. Wonder if she's free for a cannoli later?"

On my final day in Sicily—my last chance at Corleone—I walk to the ticket counter, look the clerk in the eye, and ask for a round-trip ticket to Corle—...Cefalù. Yeah, Cefalù, that's it, to see a Byzantine mosaic I remember liking in one of my schoolbooks.

Cefalù might as well have been Corleone. It had the same steep cobblestone streets and blanched little buildings that I remember from the movie. *Lovely*, I thought, as I started walking up the hill to its tiny twelfth-century cathedral. *Freak*, everyone in town apparently thought as I marched past them. An entire class of schoolchildren stopped cold to gawk at me. Six-year-old girls pointed at my shoes and laughed. Hunched old men glared, as if the sight of me was a vicious insult. I felt like a living, breathing, faux pas.

At least no one was inside the church. The only gaze upon me there came from the looming, sad-eyed Messiah. The Jesus in this mosaic is huge, three times larger than any other figure inside the church. And there's something menacing in the way he holds that tablet with the word of God on it. But his face is compassionate. With that contradictory mix of stern judgment and heart, he may as well have been wearing a tuxedo and stroking a cat and saying something like "What have I ever done to make you treat me so disrespectfully?"

I leave the church and go for lunch. I am the only patron in a tiny family restaurant operated by Mama, Papa, Son 1, and Son 2. They glare at me as if I glow in the dark. Soon they'll wish I glowed in the dark. The power keeps going on and off because of a thunderstorm. The sky outside is nearly black. The Muzak version of "A Whiter Shade of Pale" is playing and it flickers, too, so that every few seconds it's dark and silent. Which is a relief, considering that the rest of the time it's loud and the entire family have seated themselves across from me and gape without smiling. The eggplant on my plate is wonderful, but such is my desire to escape their stares that I have never chewed so fast in my life.

How had it never hit me before? The whole point of *The Godfather* is not to trust anyone outside your family. And whatever I may have thought while sitting in front of my VCR, I am not actually Sicilian. I bear no resemblance to Clemenza, Tessio, or any of the heads of the Five Families. If

I were a character in the film at all, I'd be one of those pain-in-the-ass innocent bystanders in the restaurant where Michael murders Sollozzo. I'm the tuba player in Moe Green's casino. I'm that kid who rides his bike past Michael and Kay on Kay's street in New Hampshire who yells hello and neither Michael nor Kay says hello back.

I got sucked in by *The Godfather*'s moral certainty, never quite recognizing that the other side of moral certainty is staying at home and keeping your mouth shut. Given the choice, I prefer chaos and confusion. Why live by those old-world rules? I was enamored of the movie's family ethos without realizing that in order to make a life for myself, I needed to go off on my own. Why not tell people outside the family what you're thinking? As I would later find out, it's a living.

Sarah Vowell is best known for her monologues and documentaries for public radio's "This American Life." She is the author of Radio Days, The Partly Cloudy Patriot, *and* Take the Cannoli: Stories from the New World, *from which this story was excerpted. She lives in New York.*

*

It is un-Roman, un-Christian, un-Us *not* to have gelato with whipped cream between three and five. The flavor does not matter. It is the intent, the commitment, the faithful following of The Rule that makes each day its own reward, as each day should be and is in Rome.

And after that, espresso, drunk in two sips, standing at a counter, a few lira for the java jolt flung down by Zeus. Yes, we simply must have espresso, unless...we have *granita* at an outdoor café and watch Italian men strut by.

Boldly we stare, wired into the afternoon with ice crystals of coffee shimmering darkly in a glass, layered with drifts of heavenly cream. *Granita* titillates the senses. Yes we watch the men, and whisper that our energy is shifting us in our seats. We are sirens, humming to the strutting men in tones that vibrate bone. They look at us as they pass and we all know what is going on and that it is good and simply what is done when one is having *granita* in Rome. At our age, we cannot do this every afternoon. If we were younger we would do it twice a day. We murmur about the possibility of multiple *granitas*, but we would miss the Vatican. Worse, we would miss dinner.

—Carol Stigger, "Better Than Sex"

JOANN HORNAK

Fifteen Minutes Can Last Forever

Get me out of Africa.

THE DAY THAT I NEARLY DROWNED AFTER MY RAFT flipped on rapid number one of twenty-six mostly Class V rapids, and I was sucked and held under the Zambezi River for what seemed like hours, I had assumed this was my one brush with death on my first trip to Africa. But just one week later, in pursuit of what a travel brochure had promised as the "complete safari experience," I found out how wrong my assumption had been.

I was on the final leg of a six-week tour that I'd taken with Sam, a friend from the States. We'd spent four days at Kayila Lodge, a private safari camp on the banks of the Lower Zambezi River in Zambia. We'd waited until our last day to take our first walking safari into the African bush with Rolf, our guide and host.

On the jetty over coffee that morning, Rolf, a Zimbabwean, lambasted the current political situation in his country of birth. He had no use for animal rights activists who threatened his part-time livelihood, big-game hunting. Nor did he care for those "damn liberals" who wanted to redistribute land by taking it from the white settlers and giving it back to the natives.

But I wasn't interested in Rolf's politics. Oozing testosterone, he gave the impression that a barehanded scuffle with a charging Cape buffalo or a thrashing crocodile was an everyday occurrence and just part of his job. Through his square-jawed, self-assured manner, he inspired complete confidence in everything he did from serving drinks to telling bush stories late into the starry evenings. Here was a man who could deliver me unharmed from the jaws of a carnivorous beast. In short, he was the quintessential man's man and safari guide.

> The male ego with few exceptions is elephantine to start with.
>
> —Bette Davis

But it wasn't just Rolf's masculine attributes that took away any trepidation I might have had about setting off into the African outback on foot. It was my ignorance. For some reason I had the whimsical notion that a walking safari would be similar to taking a stroll around the zoo, only the cages would be missing. The animals would certainly keep a respectful distance while I could admire them at my leisure. I couldn't possibly be in any real danger.

We set out early, driving a short distance into the bush in the Land Rover. Along the way, we met up with Warrix, a game scout for Kayila. Despite the fact that this grown man was the size of a young teenaged boy, he seemed formidable, armed with an AK-47 and two strings of ammunition strapped bandit-like across his narrow chest. He joined us for our trek.

We drove farther into the bush. Rolf stopped the jeep. He grabbed a .22 and a .50 caliber rifle from the trunk, tossing the .22 to Sam. We started walking.

I heard an elephant trumpet in the distance. We walked toward the sound to a small rise and saw fifty elephants in the clearing below us. It was exhilarating to be only several hundred feet away from these lumbering giants. I asked Rolf if the elephants knew we were there. He said they didn't know and that he'd hoped it would stay that way. Because of poaching, elephants have learned to associate the scent of humans with extreme danger.

But then the wind shifted.

One of the bull elephants caught our scent, panicked and trumpeted. Rolf whipped his head around and said only one word as we locked eyes, "Run!"

Run? What do you mean run? It took me several seconds to process the fact that I was in grave danger. The person I'd entrusted my life with, Mr. Oozing Testosterone, was clearly scared stiff. It took me another second or two to realize that three men armed with one weapon each couldn't do much against a herd of fifty stampeding elephants that can reach speeds of up to thirty miles an hour. But under the circumstances, with my options being severely limited, I ran.

As quickly as possible, we climbed over vines and roots, waded through thigh-level grass, skirted around bushes, and ducked under low-hanging branches. Rolf, in the lead, constantly ordered us to stay together but I kept falling behind. My heart was pounding and adrenaline coursed through my body. I heard them but couldn't see them. The sound of elephants trumpeting and charging through the bush is deafening.

One part of me knew they were coming after us, but another part of me refused to believe it. My mind played little games telling me that all I had to do was to run for a few minutes and then I would be perfectly safe. I ran as fast as I could, but like the classic nightmare where a monster is chasing you, I felt as though I was wading through quicksand.

We reached a clearing. Rolf screamed for us to drop to the ground. We dropped. Lying in the dirt, the ground reverberated, red dust swam through the air choking me. My heart beat against the earth. I could see the elephants just sixty feet away crashing through the underbrush.

We moved out again passing a tsetse fly trap. We were about twenty feet beyond the trap when Rolf screamed for us to run back to it. We stood next to the tattered cloth soaked in poison, suspended from two rods. Rolf was hoping that this flimsy piece of fabric would somehow mask the smell of four sweating, terrified human beings from fifty frenzied elephants with their acute sense of smell. I couldn't have felt more exposed had I appeared on the *Larry King Live* show naked.

When the thundering died down, we ran to a nearby cluster of trees. Rolf told us the herd had separated into three groups and that we were almost completely surrounded. This was information I definitely didn't need to hear at that moment since I was in a state of near-hypoxia. I did the only thing I could. I leaned my head against a tree and prayed with every fiber of my being, muttering over and over like a crazed lunatic, "Please God, don't let me die."

We had to move out again but I was frozen with fright. Rolf gripped my shoulders, pulled me towards him and held me close. It was a scene straight from a Hollywood action romance flick minus the obligatory passionate kiss and the fact that my hair was plastered to my face with sweat, my eyes bugged out with fear, and I looked like a zombie possessed.

"I know where to shoot an elephant to drop it. I've killed them before. Just stay close. But whatever you do, don't run if an elephant jumps out!" he said.

Elephants jumping out of bushes! I knew they were smart but I didn't know they were capable of hiding, lying in wait, and then launching a planned attack like a platoon of Marines.

We quietly sprinted, ducked, and tiptoed gingerly along the twenty-five-foot-high expanse of bushes, made it past, and continued on. We reached a ten-foot-tall termite mound and stopped there. Rolf said the jeep was nearby and he went off alone to get it. By this time, my emotions and the adrenaline had caught up with me and I started crying. Warrix told me I shouldn't cry because, "Madame did good."

Finally, fifteen minutes after Rolf had first ordered us to run, he drove up in the jeep. It was ten in the morning and we hadn't eaten a thing, but it seemed like the perfect time to start drinking. We each grabbed a forty-ounce Tusker from the cooler tucked under the back seat. I drank mine in about three minutes flat. It had no effect on me. I had another, not even a buzz.

At brunch an hour later, Rolf was back to his swaggering, you-call-that-a-brush-with-death self, although he'd confessed during our drinking binge that he'd had many close calls but none this close. On a scale from one to ten, with a ten described by Rolf as the four of us "looking like pieces of bacon after being gored and stomped to death," we were at nine. He'd almost shot an elephant during our ordeal so we could crawl up against the carcass to mask our smell from the rest of the herd. What a pleasant thought. Exactly how long were we supposed to stay in that position? Until the corpse began rotting and crawling with maggots? Until the vultures picked it clean? For the rest of our lives?

Many people hope for Andy Warhol's fifteen minutes of fame. But if this experience taught me anything, it's to heed the old adage, be careful what you wish for. Sometimes fifteen minutes can last far longer than you want it to.

JoAnn Hornak is a freelance writer, humorist, and recovering lawyer living in Milwaukee.

*

I advance gingerly into the shower. Priority one: do not step on a cockroach. I realize that they move fast enough to break the sound barrier, and that I'd probably need steel boots to actually crush one, but I am unwilling to take any chances at harming one of their number. The thought of millions of vengeful family members inspires in me a caution well-suited to space walks or neurosurgery.

As it turned out, I needn't have worried about the little beasties. I have, as the saying goes, bigger fish to fry.

Naked, wet, I cannot let go of the taps. I am in every aspect—thought processes, panic level, comically bulging eyes—like a drunken mariner seizing the ship's rail during a colossal storm, except considerably more undressed. Electrical current courses through my arms down to my feet. "Naaauugh," I holler, in neither Spanish nor English, reverting to the language of our Neolithic ancestors.

My boyfriend yells helpfully from the other room, "They don't bite!"

"There's electricity! In the bathroom!" Clearly the electroshock has diminished what little intellectual capacity the Kahlua and *cervezas* have left me. Only basic instincts for self-preservation permit me to liberate my hands. Torn between averting possible death and regaining a modest level of hygiene—well, I am a woman—vanity wins the day. My head is not smoking, I reason, and as long as I don't touch the taps, the current remains safely in the wall.

Clean and pondering my next move, I call out, "There's a current of electricity when I touch the taps!"

"You're imagining things."

Tell me and I shall forget. Show me and I will remember. Involve me and I will understand. A little something I learned while getting an education degree.

"How about a shower?" I offer magnanimously. "I'll leave it running for you."

—Anita Kugelstadt, "Pack Light"

ALISON WRIGHT

Love and War at the Pier Hotel

Welcome to the Outback, dah'lin.

"TRAVEL, MEET PEOPLE," THE AD READS. "BARMAID needed in Port Hedland, Western Australia.

I've never served drinks before in my life, but how hard can it be? I've certainly drunk enough to be familiar with the substance. I call and when the owner tells me he is paying $200 (Australian) a week under the table with room and board, I know it's a done deal. He informs me that the last girl has just left in tears. I foolishly neglect to ask why. He is desperate, which is why he is willing to hire me sight unseen.

"What's your name?" he asks. Now that I have been in Australia for over a year, my visa has just expired and I have to work here illegally until I can earn enough money to leave the country. I quickly remember to change my last name, "Ali Weston." Just as desperate, I find myself on a bus heading north from Perth the next day.

The packed bar is raucous and looks like a scene from the movie *Crocodile Dundee*. It was a grueling twenty-four-hour bus ride to get here, but my exhaustion evaporates as I size up the crowd. Dreadlocked Aboriginals and dust-covered men wearing filthy denim shorts nurse beers and catcall to me. I wish I were wearing a suit of armor rather than a sundress. I hoist my backpack on my shoulder and give my best don't-screw-with-me look as I stride across the room. Good Lord, they are actually beating their palms on the countertops as I walk past.

I am greeted by the bug-eyed owner slobbering on the burned-out stub of a cigar. "You can pour beer, right?"

"Of course," I tell him. O.K., so only into my mouth, but I feel this is only a small white lie. There is a tap on my shoulder and I turn around to see the man next to me promptly take a bite from his beer glass. As he chews with a smile I see from his frayed teeth that there have been many previous attempts at perfecting this party trick. *Hmmm*, I think, *this is intriguing. I'm going to have to stay here for a while.*

Port Hedland is an ugly one-street coastal mining town. Huge piles of salt line the streets, waiting to be loaded onto the barges. Red dust coats everything, including the people. It's home to mostly Aboriginals but many workers come on the ships from all over the world to work as miners, electricians, and construction workers. The main form of entertainment—well, the only entertainment—is to drink.

I am put to work immediately. The first beer I pour is for a crusty old man sitting at the end of the bar. As I hand it to him, a fist comes out of nowhere knocking his head to the side like a Popeye cartoon. "FIIIIIGHT!!!" wails the war call. Kay, who at twenty is only slightly younger than I am, is a tough "professional barmaid," and knows the drill. She drags me into the walk-in cooler with her. As we sit on a keg of beer freezing our butts off she explains that the fights, mostly between the Aboriginals and whites, are a nightly ritual. Like a bomb shelter, this is the safest place to hide out as the combatants proceed to trash the bar and beat each other to bloody pulps until the cops arrive.

The heavy-set fish-eyed owner, Henry, and his son, Mike, thrive on verbally abusing me and seem determined to see me break. They only make me more resolved to stay. I have support from the "permanent dwellers," who are here every day. "Ali, you keep pouring that beer, and we'll keep drinking it." My newfound friends don't care if my beer sloshes on the counter and is foamy. Mike scowls as he constantly sprays the bar counter with toxic insect repellent while people are eating, getting it in their food, their faces. The flies might be annoying I tell him, but it's no reason to poison the customers.

Back home bartenders may feel some responsibility for their clientele, but in this bar we are forced to serve them as long as they can keep coughing up the money for their drinks. Which often means serving people to the point of passing out. Or throwing up. In which case I am instructed to take away the beer, and replace it with a glass of water in case the police come in, making sure to still collect on the tab. Tonight one guy drinks until he spews all over the bar, at which point he thankfully passes out on the floor. After a few minutes he manages to clamber back up, yelling, "I'm hungry!" which has us all in stitches, all except for the guy who has puke on his shoes and proceeds to give him a judo chop in the face. He is down for the count once again.

This evening work is slow but steady, enough to keep me busy. Near the end of the night I am walking around the corner of the bar and there is old legless Max being strangled by some crazy red-faced local with saliva dribbling down his chin. I recognize the strangler as a regular, who has an unnerving habit of fluttering his hands constantly like a bird in flight. We've taken to placing pints of beers in front of him because we can't understand what else he might be asking for. Poor Max turns blue as he receives an almighty punch to the face forcing him to the floor. There is blood everywhere. It puts me in a very unsociable mood for the rest of the evening.

The bar continues its steady decline. I'm told the Pier Hotel is in the *Guinness Book of World Records* for being the most dangerous pub in the world. It doesn't surprise me. It's like being a voyeur on another planet, watching this cast of characters whose drunken brains are permanently addled with alcohol.

Weeks go by. There are fights every night. Not only have all the pool cues been snapped in half, rendering the pool table useless, but we have now lost all the disco equipment to barroom brawls. Despite the danger, I soon gain enough confidence to stand my ground. Sure, we have to duck when the beer bottles go whizzing by our heads, shattering into pieces against the steel-door refrigerators in back of us. But the fistfights no longer perturb us as much. The walls are full of holes that people punch out of anger and frustration, or just practice until they get to the real thing. There is a handwritten sign scribbled above the door in pencil, "Please don't hit the bar staff."

Richard, the licensee of the pub, falls off the wagon, and starts drinking again. He admits to me that he had thirteen beers in his room last night. The place is getting to all of us.

> It's not true that life is one damn thing after another—it's one damn thing over and over.
>
> —Edna St. Vincent Millay

Ross gives me some romantic reprieve from this

insanity. A fair-haired Kiwi, he is working here as an electrician. O.K., so he's a drunk, but at least he's a happy one. I find having a strapping big bodyguard boyfriend at the bar is not necessarily a bad thing. I think I have found true love in the middle of this hellhole.

This does not fare well with Hermann. Hermann the German seems to be just another harmless drunkard as he plants himself at the end of the bar asking for a beer. It's not only the drink, but the heat and isolation which turns the locals' brains into a gooey substance, or, as the Aussies affectionately describe their likes, "gone tropo."

"You're too beautiful to be hidden away here in this bar in the middle of nowhere," Hermann tells me as I place his drink in front of him.

"Don't worry," I tell him, "I don't plan to be here forever."

"Oh, you say that now young lady. Marry me. I want to take you away from all of this." He stands, waving his arm with a flourish for emphasis. I roll my eyes and walk away. I figure I must hear this about a dozen times a day from a broad spectrum of deadbeat losers staring at me with lust in their red-glazed eyes over a beer glass.

But Hermann is different. He is persistent. He returns that afternoon with a handwritten resumé as to why he would be a good husband, as he tries to sway me. I don't see millionaire on it, and he still looks like a loony old goat, so I turn him down. Then the poems and love stories start coming. His constant bellowing from the bar stool of his eternal affections is starting to embarrass, and quite frankly, scare me. As there is no longer a disco in the bar, this seems to be the new form of evening entertainment. Except that I have to put up with it all day. Every day. For a week.

One day the police walk in. Not an unusual occurrence around here, but this time they come right up to me. Oh my god, I've been found out. Actually, they inform me that they have arrested Hermann but he has escaped from jail. They have a summons (under my assumed name!) for me to testify in court. For someone who is working in the country illegally and trying to keep a low profile I am certainly getting a lot of police attention.

Ross comes to court with me. I'm nervous. Hermann keeps looking at Ross, threatening to fight him. He says he will kill for me. This is not good. I watch the long line of Aboriginals I recognize from being arrested at our bar go through their court appearances. So this is what they do all day. Then it's Hermann's turn. He pleads guilty.

"This is quite a serious offense, escaping from prison," the judge scolds him. "Would you like to tell the courtroom why you did this, Hermann?"

He whirls around the courtroom, pointing his finger directly at me.

"Because of her!" he yells. "I love her! I want to marry her and take her away from all of this!"

The whole courtroom, including the entire local police force, bursts into laughter. I feel my cheeks turning red. I am mortified. So much for being incognito.

"I understand," says the judge. "We've all fallen in love with pretty young barmaids before. But still, you have to leave her alone," he warns. He lets him off on probation. Big mistake.

Hermann pounds on my bedroom door all day and continues clamoring over me in the bar in the evening. I am furious with Henry for not banning him from the establishment. Suddenly, Henry just turns around and backhands Hermann right in the face. "And I should do the same to you for leading him on," he yells. I now realize that Henry is truly psychotic. And I quit.

A group of us go to the bar next door for drinks to let off steam. Hermann follows and tries to kill Ross with a hammer. Ross, who is the most passive person I have met in what seems forever, floors Hermann with a plastic red chair. We all make a break for my room. Hermann proves to be indestructible as he attempts to break down my door with the hammer. His frustration continues as we hear him pulling a Keith Moon, trashing the room next door in an enraged tantrum.

Finally the police pull up, taking Hermann away. This time he is to be committed to the sanitarium. We continue to do shots of tequila until dawn. The guys present me with a wad of cash they've taken up from the bar as a collection, enough to get me the hell out of this place. After seven weeks of this madness, I'm more than ready to move on. Shortly after I leave, the Pier Hotel closes down.

Alison Wright, a freelance photojournalist based in San Francisco, specializes in documenting the traditions and changes of endangered people in remote areas of the world. She has won the Lowell Thomas Award for her writing and is a recipient of the Dorothea Lange Award in documentary photography for her photographs of child labor in Asia. This work is the basis of her most current photographic book on children around the world called Faces of Hope: Children of a Changing World. *Her previous books,* The Spirit of Tibet: Portrait of a Culture in Exile *and* A Simple Monk: Writings on the Dalai Lama, *are part of a traveling photo exhibition which has been featured at the Smithsonian Institute in Washington, D.C.*

JENNIFER COLVIN

Cultural Exposure

Yes, that is *what you think it is.*

THE PROTRUDING CAUSES BROODING AND IS IN NO WAY SOOTHING TO THE MASSES...

In a plane somewhere over the Atlantic, I finished some reading from one of my last college classes. I laughed at Ted Joans's poem about supposed punishments dished out for "protruding" offenses in different countries around the world. Over the next three months as I traveled by myself through the United Kingdom, Ireland, France, Italy, and Greece, I would discover that none of these laws were being enforced in Europe.

Eventually, I'd be exposed to penises from a range of nationalities in the parks, beaches, museums, and youth hostels of Europe. But starting in the English-speaking countries, my exposure to men was inhibited by the cold March weather. All of the men I encountered in public in the U.K. were fully clothed—as would be expected. But the farther south I traveled on the European continent that spring, the warmer it got and the more I was exposed to men from other cultures.

By the time I arrived in France I needed to rely on body language to communicate. I found that pointing was a simple way to get what I wanted quickly. However, all I usually wanted was a sandwich or to know where the toilets were. Many of the men I encountered wanted something else. Afraid that anything be left to the imagination or somehow left open for misinterpretation, men would get straight to the point by pointing to, or with, their penises. It seemed that like love, the language of male exhibitionists and masturbators was an international one.

One sunny morning, I wandered through an empty park in Arles in the south of France, seeing the same grounds Vincent van Gogh had seen when he lived there. Tall trees shaded a pale dirt path that led to a quiet spot by a stream. I felt like I was walking alone through a Van Gogh painting, and I was surprised to see an older man sitting on a bench on the opposite grassy bank. I was even more surprised to see he was holding a stubby erection in his hand.

He looked up, and catching my eye across the stream, waved his penis in my direction. "*Capisce,* eh?" he said with a friendly smile, as though he were gesturing to the beautiful gardens nearby and commenting on the lovely morning.

Capisce? I thought. Why's he speaking Italian? Did he expect me to jump the stream and take things into my own hands? I wanted to reply with something witty in French, but I got so flustered that I simply left. He seemed to be contemplating peacefully, but he left me brooding. Walking back to the town center, I formulated all kinds of snappy comebacks using nearly the entire range of my limited French vocabulary but always including the word *"petit."*

On the beaches in France, I had learned to accept seeing topless women as a matter of course. It no longer seemed shocking to see breasts casually revealed, lotioned and tanned, in public. You would think that after having seen so many European men in tight, skimpy Speedos, it wouldn't come as too much of a surprise the day an older man decided to give me an anatomy lesson at a popular beach.

However, I was completely caught off guard when I looked up from the book I was reading to see a well-fed, gray-haired man strolling slowly in my direction, completely nude. Below his ample belly one of the smallest penises I had ever seen stuck nearly straight out, cushioned by his large balls. He wandered my way and stopped in front of me. With his hands on his hips, fingers pointing to his crotch, he casually surveyed the coastline.

I briefly wondered if I had unknowingly wandered onto a nude beach. Startled, I looked around to see if there were other nude men nearby. Nope, it was just this one. Relieved, I looked back at the man. What exactly was protruding? Behind the safety of my sunglasses, I tried to focus in for a closer look. Yes, it was small, but it was different somehow. That's when it hit me. For the first time, I was looking at an uncircumcised penis.

I didn't realize I had been staring for so long until the man turned away and surveyed the horizon beyond the ocean. I smiled to myself. Perhaps this would be my secret weapon: an intense gaze of confusion and curiosity might intimidate future crotch-wiggling men and exhibitionists into shielding their sausages from view. But the alternative, a back-end view, wasn't necessarily a better option.

A week later, I arrived in Italy fully prepared for an assault of male attention. I had been warned about the consequences of traveling alone in Italy as a young blonde woman, but I was determined to continue on my own. Much to my relief, most of the male nudity I was to see would be confined to the museums.

My first stop was in Florence, where I stood in line for hours in the early morning before it got too hot, waiting to visit the Galleria dell'Accademia and see Michelangelo's *David*. Once inside, most tourists walked past the other sculptures directly to the back, where *David* was displayed in all his glory. Thanks to the pedestal the statue rests on, *David* 's penis was just about at eye level. Excited tourists took turns standing next to the statue, grinning widely at a camera as friends took photos.

Their enthusiasm made me wonder what exactly they planned on doing with the pictures. Would they go in the photo album next to the picture of the family at the beach, or be put up on the refrigerator? They wouldn't frame something like that, would they?

The next incident occurred at a youth hostel in Rome. Tired after a long day of sightseeing, I sat in the narrow, worn room at the front of the youth hostel that doubled as a lounge and reception area. It was easy to strike up a conversation with the young, tan Australian reading a book nearby. We decided to play cards. Sitting across from each other, a small table between us, I quickly taught him the basics of gin. After our first practice game I realized he wouldn't be very stiff competition, but he was a good sport about losing.

At one point, while he was studying his cards and trying to figure out his next move, I thought about letting him win a game or two to boost his confidence. I leaned back in my chair, and my eyes wandered to the floor, his thong-clad feet, his tan, muscular legs, and what the hell was that?

He made his move. I sat up straight in my chair, trying desperately to maintain a poker face. I ended the game quickly just so I could shuffle the cards and give myself time to think. After dealing out another hand, I looked down and there it was again. Peeking out the bottom of his short running shorts was a limp penis. It had been there all along.

Other people came in and out of the hostel, wandered over to our table, chatted with us for a moment. Could they see it? Did they know I could see it? I won another hand. Should I tell him? Could I keep from laughing? I quickly won again and took another peek. Why did this keep happening to me? For the love of God, would I just stop looking at it?

The problem was, it seemed to be looking at me. The fact that he didn't know his penis was peeking out, combined with his ineptitude at cards, made him seem vulnerable and earnest and oddly sweet. I thought about ways to bring up the subject of his penis, but it's not an easy thing to slip into casual conversation.

I pictured a sophisticated, sexually confident version of me leaning over and whispering something clever in his ear. He would smile at me. From there, who knows? My fantasy got a little fuzzy. I didn't really want it to go much farther than that.

In reality, I knew if I said something it would be horribly awkward for both of us, and in the end, nothing would be accomplished. We'd sleep in bunk beds in the same room with ten other backpackers, and I would get up early before anyone else was awake to walk to the train station, headed to the coast to catch a ferry to Greece. I didn't say anything that night, but I thought about what might have been as I left the hostel first thing in the morning.

Arriving at the train station, I discovered I wasn't the only one who had the brilliant idea of catching the first train to

Brindisi. As I waited at the platform, hoping I could get a seat on the crowded train, I joined up with an Australian girl traveling alone. We were determined to get to Greece one way or another. Fortunately, we got there the easy way, with last-minute seats on both the train and the ferry.

After a couple drinks one night at the infamous Pink Palace in Corfu, the party place for Canadian, American, and Australian backpackers, we started telling stories about our travels. It wasn't long before the talk turned to men. I had to know, was I the only one who kept seeing penises popping up everywhere?

Soon, we were laughing as we discovered we had the same stories about overexposure to European men. We could laugh now with relief as we remembered the various nude sun bathers, unwitting "hangers-out," and occasional flashers. Protruding and brooding. The laughter was soothing.

Jennifer Colvin is a freelance writer based in Berkeley, California. When not working as a marketing professional, she spends her time scouting out surf spots while traveling by bicycle, or checking out bicycle tour routes when traveling with a surfboard.

*

That night we dined on *uccelli*, the wild birds common to the hills of Lucca, Italy. Claudio stuffed them with fragrant flowers, aromatic herbs, and homemade sausage. I had always thought Italians were heartless to eat songbirds and I eyed them suspiciously. However, my squeamishness totally disappeared with the first taste. I almost hated to confess they were delicious, especially paired with the dark red wine from last year's harvest.

These birds are a delicacy in Tuscany and can be hunted only for a short period in September and I wanted to thank Piero, the neighbor who brought them. I waxed poetic in my basic Italian, about how tasty they were, how succulent, how juicy, and how sweet the flesh, and on and on. The more I said the redder his face became.

Later, Claudio asked what I said to Piero that caused such a reaction.

I replied that I was telling him how much I enjoyed his *uccello.*

"Oh, Jacqueline, you didn't say *uccello* did you? Cara, the little birds are *uccelli*—with an "i" on the end. *Uccello* is a Tuscan slang word for penis!"

—Jacqueline Harmon Butler, "Italian Lessons"

ANNALISA VALENTINE

Pissed Off in Nepal

The bond between a mother and son-in-law is golden.

IT'S GOING TO GET WARMER. IT'LL START TO FLOW ANY minute. I hate those first few lukewarm moments of a shower, before the hot kicks in. It's been three weeks since my last shower. I anticipate the luxurious hot flow and do what over 50 percent of Americans do in the shower. I begin to pee.

Something is wrong. My eyes pop open. I'm peeing in my down sleeping bag. But the shower is real. My hat, gloves, and sweaty clothing are hanging from a light line that I've strung across the top of my sleeping space. The water is dripping from the top bunk onto my gloves, then running down each finger and onto my face.

I try to scoot to the side, but I am packaged alongside fifteen Germans. We share a shelf-like bottom bunk, each occupant allotted eighteen inches of territory. We are all miserable. The one true sleeper alternates five short snorts on the inhale with a long, slow vibration of mucoid throat streamers on the exhale. My kids, Lori and David, and Lori's fiancé, Mike, are in the bunk above me. I scoot towards the foot of my territory, my feet extending over the end.

We started our trek in Jiri, nearly a month ago. This was David's choice. I had offered him "Anywhere in the World" for his master's degree celebration. I was ecstatic that he chose to stand in the glory of Mt. Everest. Lori and Mike had spent the month of March attending the teachings of the Dalai Lama in Dharamsala, India, then joined David and me in Kathmandu. They announced their engagement to us on April Fools' Day, the first day of the trek.

Now we're in Lobuche. Sixteen thousand feet above sea level. A few small tea houses, each with a sitting room, a two-bunk dormitory room, and a toilet-free outhouse. The outhouse cubicles have only a floor. But two of the floorboards are wide enough apart to allow you to eliminate between them. Bring your own paper and for God's sake, don't drop anything.

We split up early this morning for summit day. Lori and Mike wanted to visit Base Camp, David and I chose to climb the Kala Patar summit. At this altitude, 18,400 feet, there's half as much air as at sea level. Half as much oxygen. Each cotton candy breath was full of sweet promise, and then empty. One step, three breaths, one step, three breaths. This was my mantra as I slowly ascended the mountain. David plodded patiently behind me.

Mt. Everest stayed hidden behind Nuptse, a foreground peak, until the moment we stepped upon the Kala Patar summit. David and I stood together in awe. We could sense, see, feel, even hear Mt. Everest, another 10,000 feet above us, her rocky peak piercing the jet stream, creating a windstorm that appeared as a hat, tilting off her head. The frigid air of her glaciers penetrated the dry, sunny Kala Patar summit. I was dwarfed by the magnitude. I cried as the summit fed straight to my hungry soul.

The hike back to Lobuche seemed to go on forever. By dusk, Lori and Mike had still not returned from their trip to

Base Camp. Just after dark they staggered in. Mike was leaning heavily on Lori. Both were crying. Both feared that he was going to die.

They had spent most of the day trudging along the Khumbu Glacier towards Base Camp. They weren't finding it. Lori started getting scared. The glacier seemed to be moving, she could hear water flowing and pebbles tumbling underfoot, and it was snowing too hard for them to find the trail markers. As Mike had encouraged her to tough it out, he was suddenly hit by a debilitating headache. He was unable to see, and barely able to walk. She had slowly led him back the six hours to Lobuche.

The only cure for the incapacitating headache of altitude sickness is descent to a lower elevation. But a six-hour hike, in a snowstorm, in the dark is pretty perilous as well, especially when it was Mike who really knew the trail. You can live for a little while with cerebral edema. It's pulmonary edema, when your lungs fill with water, that kills you quickly. We decided to stay at Lobuche until four A.M., and then try to evacuate Mike to a lower elevation. Before going to bed, we had each packed our bags, so we would only need to stuff in our sleeping bags to hit the trail.

Now this. Four more hours till dawn. I've scooted away from the dripping, but a puddle is developing at my head. And the middle of my bag is a big wad of wet feathers. I guess I can't ignore it any longer. I fumble with my feet to capture my headlamp at the bottom of my sleeping bag. I secure it on my head and work the moist zipper open. The night air is freezing. The Germans rearrange themselves. I worm my way to the foot of my sleeping slot, and pull myself up to peer into the upper domain, careful not to let my feet near the filthy wet floorboards.

At first sweep of the flashlight beam, I see no cause for

alarm. Fifteen sleeping bags, all in a row. Small heaps of dirty clothing wadded up for pillows. Comatose campers. I focus my search on Lori's territory, directly above mine. The beam bounces off something reflective leaning against the wall at her head. Why would she have a ratty old zip-lock bag, half full of liquid? I check the ceiling. Nothing suspicious. I return the beam to the zip-lock. A lemony glint in the reflection, and the sickening truth dawns.

"Jesus Christ. You're pissing on me. Give me that fucking bag." My whispered hiss is amplified by the empty air.

All fifteen of the inhabitants of the upper bunk, including Mike, burst out laughing. This is a good sign that maybe he is recovering. He had been so crazy with pain that he was unable to move. He had drunk a lot of water because hydration is the best antidote to altitude sickness, and of course, with hydration comes the need to pee. As David and twelve other trekkers listened and waited, Lori had removed her snacks from a one-quart zip-lock bag, and somehow accomplished the feat of having Mike let his bladder into the bag. She did not completely succeed in the sealing of the bag, however. At least half had dribbled onto me.

I placed the leaking bag on the floor, and spent the rest of the night wet and angry. As we packed up for our descent at daybreak, Mike's headache had subsided somewhat, and he was able to absorb the full pain and humiliation of having pissed on his future mother-in-law.

Annalisa Valentine has co-piloted a shrimp boat to Alaska, researched coral reefs in Mexico, filmed the horrible conditions of women in Sudan, crewed on the Biosphere's research vessel in the Red Sea, been taken captive in Eritrea, and deported from India. When she is not traveling she calls home Santa Cruz, California and Los Barriles, Mexico.

LESLEY QUINN

At a Loss for Words

Mothers know best…or do they?

AFTER ALMOST FIVE WEEKS OF SUSTAINED CLUELESSNESS, my ability to remain cheerful in the face of continuing humiliation was wearing thin, and how comforting it was to realize English would soon be the default language. My thirteen-year-old daughter Molly and I had only to cope with French for another hour.

Every year at the beginning of August, the inhabitants of Paris abandon their city in huge flocks, like migrating birds, for the entire month. I knew this—everyone knows this—but I wasn't prepared for the scene that awaited us at the airport. Out of the taxi, with stuffed shopping bags atop a rolling suitcase for every available hand, Molly and I stepped directly into an ocean of Parisians. People stood shoulder-to-shoulder, hundreds deep, in purposeful but, to us, entirely baffling formations. Polite questions in English were met with irritated discharges of cigarette smoke, and the usual impenetrable French.

I'd have started whimpering myself if Molly hadn't beaten me to it. "Mom, where are we supposed to *go*?"

"Let's try this one," I said, stepping confidently into line behind an excessively perfumed older woman in zebra mules. Right away I felt a vigorous tap on my shoulder and beheld a hostile forefinger pointing to a far end of the terminal where, I now understood, I'd find the *end* of the line.

After we had rid ourselves of all but our unwieldy carry-on bags, we fought our way to the remote departure gate where, I figured, I'd find a place to buy a book written in English. But after walking what seemed at least five miles along a series of movable sidewalks, what I found was one useless duty free perfume shop.

Uh oh. Not even with pharmaceutical assistance could I survive the next seventeen hours of airplane travel without a book.

We were to board in thirty minutes. I had to make a quick decision. If Molly and I both returned to the main terminal, with our ludicrous carry-on luggage and our shredded shopping bags, we'd have to wait in the long security line a second time. Clearly, we'd never make it.

I took a deep breath.

"Listen Molly," I began in my most Mary Poppins voice. "You're going to wait here with our stuff, okay? I'm just going to run back and grab a book. Real quick."

"What?" she said, all the blood draining from her face.

"It'll be fine," I assured her calmly. "We'll find a nice person for you to wait with."

"No way, Mom."

"You are thirteen years old now—you're practically an adult, Molly. You can do this, really, you can. It's time to grow up! I'll be right back. Fifteen minutes, max."

"No," she said firmly. "Absolutely *not*. What if the plane leaves without you? I'm sticking with you. That's just the way it is, Mom. I'm very sorry."

"Listen," I hissed. "I *must* find a book! I'm begging you. Look at my eyes. Can't you see that I will go *insane* if I don't have a book? There isn't time for us to schlep all these bags all the way back to the bookstore. I will—"

"Mom! No!"

"—run the whole way there and the whole way back. I will buy you the new *Teen People Magazine*. I will buy you *several* teen magazines. I will get gum—not sugar free! I will get chocolate. I will pay you any amount of money you require, but *you have to do this* for me. Please, Molly. This is really, *really* important."

"Mom? You don't seem to be *hearing* me? I'm afraid—"

"Let's go," I said, dragging her by the elbow toward the first person in the waiting area old enough to be a grandmother. Better still, the woman spoke English. I exchanged rushed and insincere pleasantries before I shoved Molly in Granny's direction. To my relief the woman smiled at Molly and patted the empty seat beside her.

"Okay!" I shouted over my shoulder, disregarding the look of panic on Molly's face, not to mention the outraged stares of our fellow passengers. "I'll be right back!"

Off I dashed back toward the first moveable sidewalk, only to discover it was blocked with out-of-service yellow tape. Undeterred, I flew down the first rubberized ramp. I muscled and squeezed past slow-movers, I pushed and pardoned my way to the second movable sidewalk (it was working!) and sprinted on in the fast lane with superhuman speed.

No English books in the first shop. My lungs burned but on I ran past cheese shops, record shops, the Louvre shop, my leather sandals slapping on the marble floors until, *thank you Jesus!*, a small stand of English books! A rack of trashy American magazines even.

Okay. First, a book. Robert Ludlum...Danielle Steele... John Grisham...Dick Francis. Could I dare hope for something less distasteful? To my immense relief, out of this sea of bad books rose John Irving's *A Widow for One Year*. I snatched a copy and turned to load both arms full of adolescent magazines before racing toward check out.

So far, so good. A few remaining francs and just enough time to score the new Ricky Martin CD I'd seen in a passing window.

I'm a terrible mother, I thought as I stuffed the CD into my purse and fought my way back to the long line of travelers at security. She'll never forgive me, and who could blame her? She's probably weeping in the arms of a complete stranger at this moment. *That's* the memory of France she'll carry into adulthood. I shoved my way to the front of the line, impervious to looks of annoyance and murmurs of reproach. I cut in front of the old and infirm and pushed my way back onto the movable sidewalk.

Finally, I fell gasping and triumphant at Molly's feet, sweat pouring down my beet-red face. I heaped my purchases into her lap, symbols of my everlasting gratitude.

"Here," I said.

At the first sight of Ricky Martin, her narrowed eyes softened and some color returned to her cheeks. "Where's the chocolate?" she asked.

"We will now begin pre-boarding families with children," came the announcement overhead. I lavished quick praise upon Granny—who sported, I suddenly noticed, tattooed knuckles and a nose-ring—as I began gathering up our things.

"Wait a minute, Mom. What are you doing? *I'm* not a child," Molly said. "They called people with *children*."

"What, are you kidding?" I whispered, pushing her to the front of the line. "You're only thirteen for god's sake! Anyway, you're small. Let's go."

Lesley Quinn is a freelance writer and editor living in the San Francisco Bay Area. Her work, in addition to being foisted upon unsuspecting friends of her mother, has appeared in The New York Times, Brain, Child, *and* Skirt! Magazine. *She can be reached at* lesley@qua.com.

*

I drool at the weekly published airfare sales, long to feel the humidity of Bangkok, and taste fish tacos in Mexico. So you would think that I would have no trouble accompanying my mother on an all-expenses-paid trip to England. But I do. I really do. For two reasons. First, I have already been there, twenty years ago with my elderly grandfather. A disastrous trip, where I spent a week bandaging his backside (he had a boil removed from his buttocks two days before we left), hand-washing what few clothes he had (the airline lost his luggage), and developing an ulcer. Secondly, my mother's health is less than stellar, as she comes equipped with a pacemaker *and* a built-in defibrillator, as well as two very bad knees that need reconstruction, making any type of meaningful foot travel impossible. Oh, and thirdly, her idea of a dream trip is visiting all that screams tourist—Buckingham Palace, the Crown Jewels, Big Ben, Westminster Abbey...you get the picture. So what's a girl to do?

—Susan Brady, "The Joys of Travel"

KELLY SIMON

A Family Connection

When nature calls, get off the phone.

CHATTERING RAPID GREEK INTO THE MOUTHPIECE, THE pretty mother leans against the wall of the phone kiosk, the receiver pressed to her ear. Her small sons play close by, dressed in rubber sandals and scant bathing trunks of brilliant crimson, the color in sharp contrast with the ancient biscuit-toned buildings stained black with Corfu mildew. The youngest, around two, kneels on the sidewalk poking at a bug with a twig. The elder, fourish, peers into a crumpled cigarette package retrieved from the gutter.

The mother talks on, now smiting her forehead, now waving her hands. Every few moments, she sweeps her mass of chestnut hair to the opposite side, her organdy dress billowing like wings with the extravagance of her gestures. I have been waiting for twelve minutes for her to finish with the phone so I can call home. I wander away for a few minutes, hoping my absence will spur her to finish her conversation whose gist—as far as I can make out—is the retelling of a friend's husband's most recent infidelity.

The streets are narrow and winding, shouldered with shops selling staples like fruit-scented ball-point pens and t-shirts bearing such slogans as, "I LOST IT IN CORFU." Menu boards boast British breakfasts—"HEINZ BAKED BEANS AND ENGLISH TEA." Proprietors tug at my hand, pleading, "You come my s'op."

"Mam-ma, Mam-ma," the older child squeals frantically as I return ten minutes later to a scene not much different from the one I left, except that the younger child has tugged his trunks to his knees and is now working them down around his ankles. Finally, he steps out of them exposing a bottom as white as risen dough. The mother turns a half turn, shutting the naked child from her view.

"Mam-ma, Mam-ma," the older one calls again, a hysterical edge to his voice. But either the mother does not hear, or refuses to, and continues with her animated conversation, gesticulating wildly, invoking heaven. The older brother slumps on the curb tearing at his hair as the baby squats and relieves himself on the sidewalk, leaving behind a steaming little pile. The baby waddles over to his mother and tugs gently at her dress. The mother brushes his hand away. He reaches up, grabs hold of the diaphanous garment and yanks at it, trying to get her attention. She swats his hand away and jabbers on, raking her mane back from her forehead with laquered fingertips.

With a sigh, the baby crumples a handful of her dress and wipes his bottom with the gossamer cloth. Duty done, he turns his attention to something glittery in the sidewalk. He crawls over to investigate it, his mother's dress caught fast between the cheeks of his buttocks, stretching taut the fabric as she chatters on, connected to her offspring by the umbilicus of her hem.

Kelly Simon's work has been broadcast on National Public Radio and has appeared in a wide range of publications, including The Quarterly, Ellery Queen Magazine, The Washington Post, *and* Ploughshares. *She lives in San Francisco.*

KATE CRAWFORD

Learning to Think Outside a Parisian Box

You've got the key to my heart…where is it again?

IT WAS PARIS, I WAS YOUNG AND IN LOVE WITH LIFE AND Paris, if not with Alain Chausse. Or was that Chausse Alain? I never knew, until the morning I became Madame Chausse.

My friend Joan was letting me camp on the floor of the room she traded for twice-weekly English lessons to the owner's children. It was a maid's room on the fourteenth floor of a *belle époque* building. The family lived on the fifth. The elevator stopped on the ninth.

Out our window, whose sill acted as our refrigerator, we could see the slates and the tiles, the gargoyles and angels of Paris's roofs. They boxed in a hummock of treetops and the distant dome of a Gothic cathedral. In my memory every view of Paris that year was gorgeous. The room was not. Joan had a single army-camp bed, one table, one straight-back chair, a built-in cabinet, and a hand-washing sink. My air mattress, when inflated, took up the whole floor. If Joan got up, I got up. Our toilet—two foot marks, one hole—was up one flight and down the hall. We swam at an American Club when sponge baths no longer passed muster.

My *raison d'être* was to learn French. I studied at the Alliance Française with the other beginning students from Japan, Germany, Scandinavia, and Africa. On the whole, I didn't understand them, they didn't understand me, and none of us understood Madame, our instructor. She called on me with vicious regularity, not because I was clever, but because I made her laugh. Madame thought my accent was hilarious. She explained that whenever the French want to be *really* funny, they speak with an American accent.

My progress was not encouraging, but I could hardly blame Madame. This was—including eighth grade, high school, and college—my fourth go at beginning French. I had *Le Balloon Rouge* down pat, but was terminally stuck on verbs outside the immediate moment. It was a dandy way to stay in the *now*, but it was a formidable obstacle to setting forth intent and reflecting on the past.

The best way to learn a language, I'd heard, was to have an affair with a native speaker, one who didn't speak English. Clearly, I needed a new approach and this one did have a certain sex appeal. I gave it a try.

He was, I recall, rather cute—tall, blond, soulful eyes. Perhaps not an intellectual powerhouse, but given our linguistic limitations, I had no way of knowing. I wasn't even sure of his name. I'm sure he'd told me, but I'd forgotten. By the time I knew it was a name I should know, it was rather too late to inquire. I rummaged through the papers on his desk and found both Alain Chausse and Chausse Alain, but neither had commas.

We both liked red wine and Bob Dylan. We smooched along the Seine, loafed about cafés, and partied with his friends. He spoke little English and my French did improve—but it still had a long way to go. It became my habit to spend the occasional night at his place.

Compared to Joan's room, Chausse/Alain's was grand. It featured an easy chair and a small refrigerator. The toilet was just down the hall and the floor had enough space for at least three air mattresses. It was on the top of a nine-story building and had only one flaw—no elevator.

On this occasion, Chausse/Alain had departed before dawn for a three-day trip, leaving me to prepare myself for another arduous day of being ridiculed. Dressed only in monsieur's undershirt, I popped out for a quick trip down the hall. I returned to find the wind had blown the door closed. It was locked.

I pulled down the t-shirt, grateful it reached below my butt, and tried to make a plan. Even if I had known his name, I had no way to reach Chausse/Alain. Joan didn't have a phone and, as might be expected, I could not remember her French family's name. My only idea to avoid a long, t-shirt-clad, and barefooted march through Paris was to enlist the assistance of the building's concierge—a woman not known for her friendly ways. I descended the nine flights of stairs, tugged down monsieur's t-shirt, and sheepishly knocked on her door. It opened a crack.

"Oui," snapped Madame Concierge, a youngish, bullish-looking woman with black hair drawn straight back.

"Wind close door," I said in French with exaggerated wind-close-door gestures, hoping they and my funny American accent might win her over.

"Oui," she said, unsmiling.

I continued with more wild gestures and sorry French.

"Ah, *je compris*, Madame Chausse," she said, indicating she understood and motioned for me to wait. She returned with an ancient wooden box of keys about the same size as the big baby boy she had perched on her other hip.

"Oh, *merci, merci,*" I cried, forcing a smile. I took the box and lugged it up the nine flights, which did, in fact, get dramatically steeper after the fifth floor.

The box was filled with literally hundreds of keys. First, I eliminated the long-shafted, curlicued, antique keys that might have unlocked the Bastille. Then, I eliminated the tiny keys for padlocks and safes. That left an encouraging two or three hundred Yale-type keys to try. Key-dither-discard, key-dither-discard, it was like a koan. I contemplated Alain's name now that I knew it was Alain Chausse and not Chausse Alain. I reflected on how very French, and very worldly it seemed to me, to automatically call me "Madame Chausse" even though we both knew I was not. Key-dither-discard, key-dither-discard. I held out hope till the last dither, but not one key fit. I loaded them back into the box and plodded down to report to Madame Concierge.

"*Oui*, Madame Chausse," she said with a sigh when I'd made myself understood.

She was not amused and I could tell she didn't believe me. She shifted her baby to her other hip, I shifted the box to my other hip and we slogged up to Alain's door. Madame Concierge began to repeat the key-dither-discard koan. While she dithered, I ruminated and the afternoon sun streamed through the skylight overhead. *Voilà*! The answer was not in the box. It was over my head and had been there all the time. The wind that blew the door shut in the first place came through Alain's open skylight. If I could get up to the hall's skylight, a quick trip over the roof would let me drop right into his room.

Madame Concierge, already tired dithering, agreed to this new approach. So, the baby, the box, the concierge, and I trudged back down to retrieve a ladder; and then the baby, the ladder, the concierge, and I struggled back up, stopping to gasp for breath on each landing.

Madame would not let me on the ladder, fearing, no doubt, she'd end up with both me and my broken leg on her hands. So, I sang "Frère Jacques" to her screaming baby, but quit when I decided the song might be his problem. I just held my breath. Madame made her ascent and, *merci dieu*, she made it. I thanked her repeatedly as she came out Alain's door. I dragged the ladder back down the stairs, limped up the now K2-steep nine flights, threw on my clothes, and shot out of there.

At the nearest chocolatier, I bought a chocolate for myself and a box for Madame Concierge. I returned to the scene and gave her the chocolates.

"*Oui,* Madame Chausse," was all she said.

Kate Crawford currently lives in Sebastopol, California, and is beginning to think the time may be ripe for another French intensive.

*

Slamming the dryer down on the sink, I pull on a pair of jeans and a t-shirt, run a comb through my hair, and go down to the lobby to fetch Early Riser, who is neither at the magazine rack, nor in the breakfast room. Nor is he at his usual default position, fiddling with the dials in the telephone *cabine*. In fact, he is nowhere in sight, and in that instant, I realize that he has the key and I am locked out of the room.

A managerial-looking fellow in a dark suit and a frown to match is bearing down on me. "*Per favore*," I say, trying to sound like Princess Grace might if her hair were dripping down the front of her shirt like wet fusilli. "*Ha visto mi marito*?" "He went that way," I think he says, pointing down the *lungomare*. "Would you mind letting me in?" "*Scusi*?" he says. "I would like access," I mean to say, but, the instant the words are out, I realize I have requested an abcess.

—Kelly Simon, *"La Doccia Vita"*

CHRISTINE MICHAUD

Chador Etiquette

Beauty is custom made.

DARKNESS HAD FALLEN ON THE QUIET BAY ALMIGHTY Saddam once set ablaze for months on end. All across the city, muezzins perched atop neon-lit minarets were calling believers to prayer, their blaring chants echoing off into desert and sea. The timing was perfect. Hugging a black cloak around me, I slipped out into the warm winter night.

A few blocks from the nearest mosque, four women walking closely together passed me by. In addition to the standard chador—a large black cloak and head covering—they wore a black gauze that completely covered their faces and gloves that forbade any sight of their hands. Like black ghosts, they silently floated away down the narrow alley, leaving but the scent of their expensive perfume to be remembered. Tonight, I had decided to be one of them. Having similarly concealed my alienating fairness under silky veils, I could be just another black ghost in the land of Allah.

Or I could make an all-time fool of myself.

It all happened a few days after I first set foot in Kuwait, a country a single woman cannot enter unless she is visiting blood relatives, a husband, or going on business. My boss had worked miracles to get me in, as I had been refused entry to other Gulf countries such as Qatar where officials insisted that the sole business purpose of an unmarried blond girl in the region should be prostitution!

By then I had seen the Arabian desert, crowds of sheikhs in golden-trimmed robes, and a whole lot of Mercedes. However I had yet to visit any of the expensive malls dotting the city. And so on this lonely evening, I decided to venture beyond the limits of my regular hotel-to-office route to go shopping. I was leaving the business center. Alone. Time had now come to take out Jihan's chador.

Jihan was the wife of an Arab co-worker who had kindly offered to teach me the fundamentals of proper veiling. While only Saudi authorities demand that foreign women cover up, I figured one could never be too prepared. Thus, a few days before I left for the Arab Gulf, I dropped by Jihan's place for my initiation to modesty.

A shy Filipino maid answered the door and ushered me to a posh living room where Jihan greeted me with three kisses. Jihan was a tiny Saudi woman in her early thirties. She wore a white sweater and blue jeans that matched her tight navy *hijab*—a headscarf worn by Muslim women to conceal hair and neck. On the wall before me hung a large framed picture portraying Jihan and her husband in a romantic embrace. He wore a three-piece suit and she a white *hijab* that matched her dress.

After a mandatory tea and round of questions about the most current health status of each of my family members, Jihan invited me to follow her into her lavish bedroom for "the lesson." She pulled a number of sweetly perfumed silk scarves out of a fancy drawer and laid them out on the gigantic bed for me to make my selection.

Jihan stressed the importance of a well-centred *hijab* (pronounced "*hee-djab*"), drawing my attention to the discreet ironed-in ply that marked the center of each scarf and was meant to be aligned with my nose. She swiftly took off her own *hijab* and proceeded to address me with step-by-step instructions while skillfully covering back up her thick black mane.

A *hijab* looks deceivingly easy to put on, especially when you receive instructions from a woman who has been wearing one for twenty years. Basically, the Muslim head covering is nothing but a large square of cloth folded once into a triangle. The fold goes over the forehead and the sides are pinned tightly under the chin to completely cover a woman's hair, ears, and neck. One of the tips of the scarf is then wrapped around the neck to hide the unfashionable pin.

Now, how hard can this be? Well, for someone who's got a perfect cube for a head, I suppose it's a cinch. For the rest of us sporting somewhat rounded skulls, no *hijab* will ever fit tightly and entirely hide a full hairline unless it is slightly folded in on each side just above ear level, symmetrically of course.

While I could achieve symmetrical folds, closing a safety pin under my chin single-handedly (the other hand is busy holding the whole thing tight) was simply beyond my poor Catholic girl's capacities.

"You might need a little practice," Jihan told me, unable to conceal a smile as I furiously struggled with my safety pin in a vain attempt to cover up one last unruly blond lock. Leaving me looking more like a desert warrior than a modest lady, Jihan disappeared into the depths of her walk-in closet and re-emerged with a chador in hand.

She gently took the pin out of my clumsy fingers, expertly rearranged my rebellious headgear and secured it tightly under my chin. She then helped me put on the chador and had me turn to the full-length mirror.

"A chador calls respect," she said talking to my reflection. "Although you are not required to wear it, it'll make it easier for you to go unnoticed."

Easier for me to go unnoticed? I'm a husky five-foot-nine, blue-eyed blonde with chipmunk cheeks and a little curled up nose. That made me twice the size of Jihan with half her pigmentation. A total chameleon.

I thanked Jihan profusely as she carefully folded "my" black *hijab* and chador into a plastic bag. I could give both back whenever I returned, she insisted. Jihan accompanied me to the door, kissed me three times and wished me luck.

And may Allah watch over me.

In spite of my protests, the borrowed outfit was meticulously sprayed with holy water by my I-don't-feel-this-trip-is-a-good-idea-and-I-still-think-you-should-dye-your-hair-brown mother. Candles were lit and prayers were said for me all over the province.

And may God bless me.

The scorching sun was setting quickly over a skyline of towers and slender minarets. I knew Kuwaitis would soon pour out of their air-conditioned hideouts to enjoy the evening's relieving coolness. And so would I.

I pulled Jihan's silk chador and *hijab* from the bottom of my suitcase, pleased to find them both surprisingly wrinkle-free. Remembering the little Saudi lady's detailed instructions, I proceeded to wrap up my blond head the Arab way.

Unfortunately, no matter what I did, the silky scarf slipped back, forth, and sideways over and again. My uneven folds took turns coming loose and I completely lost sight of that center ply. After nearly slashing my jugular open with the pin, I had to face the facts: I couldn't put on a *hijab* decently if my life depended on it.

So much for the *hijab*, I decided, the chador would have to do. Throwing the silk cloak over a long black skirt and black top, I headed on out to my fancy mall.

The mall was really nothing to rant and rave about, at least not for someone who had been expecting golden elevators, crystal chandeliers, and wall-to-wall Persian carpets. Bare grey floors of composite marble, white gypsum walls, and neon lights were all I found. Sure, it was airy, new and modern, but in a disappointingly American way. Nonetheless, the mere fact of having a chador on made me happy, so I went on with my window shopping.

> The sign on the temple read HINDUS ONLY. In order to appease my obvious disappointment, a young Hindu kid said to me, "Don't worry, in your next life, you'll come back a Hindu and can go into the temple."
>
> —Mary Noble, "First Time in Asia"

Yet the more I walked around, the more I got the uneasy feeling that everyone was intensely staring at me. First resorting to denial, I discarded the feeling as the product of a CNN-bred paranoia.

The stares persisted throughout the mall. After the fifteen most self-conscious minutes of my life, I finally noticed that most women wore their chador pulled over the head, much like one does when pulling their coat over them in the rain. After a week in Kuwait, it made perfect sense to me that the curve of a woman's neck would be considered too provocative a sight and had to be concealed under yet another veil.

"So that's what it is, I'm wearing this thing like a tourist," I thought to myself. Jihan had never been to Kuwait, maybe she didn't know about this local trend.

I pulled the chador over my head.

The stares doubled and children started pointing at me. Now there was no mistaking: there was something distinctively odd about me and it was entertaining the mall's entire clientele. What was these people's problem anyway? I was all covered up like everybody else, what more did they expect me to do? I just didn't get it.

Then I walked by a full-length mirror.

Jihan was a full nine inches shorter than me. Pulled up over my head as it now was, her chador barely covered my butt. What the whole mall was staring at was some freaky cross between E.T., Thor, and the Flying Nun.

But that was only half the story.

The Koran preaches that women should "*not strike their feet so that what they hide of their ornaments may be known*" (The Light, 24.31). In plain English, this means a gal shouldn't walk in a fast heavy pace because it makes her boobs jiggle.

Indeed, there is much more to wearing a chador than putting it on. I later learned—and witnessed—that a woman veiled from head to toe can actually be incredibly sensual, and sometimes outright sexy. The secret lies in the way she makes her veils flow about her when she walks. Her body will move in harmony with wind and light to let her soft silky robes flow sensually with her every step. Speed—or lack of—is therefore key.

Some veiled women even wear little bells around their hidden ankles and literally stop traffic when they stroll across busy intersections in a walking melody. Women the world over have an intrinsic need to please; veiled ladies have simply found their own way of being beautiful.

In light of all this, I could only be damned. Being as graceful and light-footed as my lumberjack grandfathers, there was nothing to do but accept that no number of veils could ever make me pass for a "believing woman."

The short but intense episode of horror that followed the sight of my own grotesque reflection only served to entertain the mall crowd some more. Without further ado, I tore the ludicrous black cloak off my head and back and I shoved it in my purse. As I stormed out of the mall through a forest of giggling black ghosts, Jihan's words echoed through my mind: "A chador calls respect...it'll make it easier for you to go unnoticed...easier for you to go unnoticed."

Don't be fooled: all black ghosts were not created equal. Some are definitely spookier than others.

Christine Michaud is allegedly a direct descendant of Erik the Red. She inherited both his temper and spirit of adventure, albeit not the ability to keep her breakfast down at sea. Her stories on Latin America, the Middle East, and Europe have appeared on www.bootsnall.com. Christine stores her backpack and orthopedic insoles in Montreal.

ADAIR LARA

What to Wear

Chic in travelspeak.

I NEVER PACK MY OWN SUITCASE WHEN I'M GETTING ready for a trip. I pack for somebody else entirely. The person I pack for is someone I hardly recognize, but I can tell from what she's taking that she's somebody I'd like to be.

We are going to Indonesia for three weeks, and I just threw in a khaki wraparound skirt for the warm afternoons. That's how I know I am somehow packing for someone else: I wear skirts to my own weddings, and that's pretty much it. I'm like my sister Adrian, who did consent to get married in a dress, but had a rolled-up pair of jeans in her purse for afterward.

I own several skirts, though, and the person I am packing for appears to be taking those, even the black "kicky" skirt that is perhaps a tiny bit wrong for the equator, and a long black dress. She even tossed in a baggie containing a sparkly necklace with matching dangly earrings.

I envy her that—I've always wanted to be able to wear those eye-catching, shoulder-grazing earrings that other women do, rather than my training-wheel versions, tiny little I'm-not-really-wearing-earrings stubs of color.

And she is chic: I can tell from this pair of tiny strapless sandals I'm putting in that she strides across the world's surfaces in pretty shoes. I myself go everywhere in the same pair of battered green hiking sandals or risk a pair of weepy feet.

She's also taking a cute red belt, instead of leaving her tops hanging loose. And—aha!—this filmy night stuff. I have some identical to it that Bill bought me, but I'm waiting to feel right about my body before I wear it for him. This woman has no such problems with body image. There the stuff is, bold as brass.

> The worst part of being a woman is the handbag. And I should know. I have hundreds of them. Big ones, small ones, clutches, zipper closures, Velcro jobbies, ones with feathers, rhinestones, ribbons, knock-offs, real deals, bags made from leather, nylon, reptile skin, canvas, and silk. I believe seasons change so I can buy a new bag without feeling too guilty—it's not that I want a new purse, it's that I need one, if only to keep up with vacillating weather trends.
>
> —Robin Epstein, "My Handbag, My Self"

But then she appears to be considerably thinner than I am, able to wear the shorts and little tops that make me want to suck my stomach in constantly. She appears to be a girl of the type I've always wanted to be, wearing heels and tight skirts and able to not only buy eyeliner but, presumably, put it on.

She is a serious reader, eagerly seeking new information. Here's a copy of *Tristram Shandy* and one called *Flaubert's Parrot,* and several guidebooks. She won't be needing any novels, the kind you collapse with on the upper deck, with the sun on your legs and a drink in your hand.

She prefers to put her vacation time to better use than that. It's clear from these guidebooks under the lingerie that she takes an alert interest in her surroundings. I myself have trouble keeping my mind on those dense little paragraphs packed with dates. My own idea of getting ready for a destination is to steep myself in novels set there. My idea of getting ready to visit Indonesia, for example, was to read Joseph Conrad's *Outcast of the Islands* and Charles Corn's enthralling *Distant Islands*, not the Lonely Planet guide.

I've always packed like this, not only for trips, but for moves. When I started college, I imagined myself living in a little room in San Francisco's Sunset District, reading poetry down by the beach. This was far from how I usually spent my time, but I would be different, living in the city and going to school.

When I went to live in Paris I brought along a stiff leather coat that reached to my calves and cost half the money I had made working as a banquet waitress at Dominic's Restaurant. I thought that walking Parisian boulevards would turn me into the kind of person who would wear that coat.

Somehow it never turns out like that. I never wore that unwieldy coat once. And I have an idea that when I get to Indonesia, I'll rummage through this strangely packed suitcase, searching desperately for my Nike sandals, for my storybooks and jeans. Halfway across the world, and I keep running into myself.

Adair Lara is an award-winning newspaper columnist for the San Francisco Chronicle. *She is the author of several books, including* Slowing Down in a Speeded-Up World, Hold Me Close, Let Me Go *and* The Best of Adair Lara. *Her articles and essays have appeared in* Redbook, Ladies Home Journal, Parenting, Good Housekeeping, Reader's Digest, *and other national publications. She lives in San Francisco.*

⋆

On a one-year trip abroad, six months of which were spent in Southeast Asia, I made the mistake of packing just one bra, and only five pairs of undies. Not seven (for each day of the week), not thirty (for each day of the month), not, God forbid, twelve (dare I say for each month of the year), but five. Five!? Were my panties thinking they'd have weekends off? Did I think they were made of steel-reinforced cotton?

Quickly into my trip, I realized that for one year, five pairs would not suffice. O.K., you say, Hello! Buy some more. Well I was in Asia, where as a womanly-shaped North American with hips that could squirt out triplets, and curves that would make Marilyn Monroe look like she'd been following the Ally McBeal eating regime, underwear, *gaunch, smalls*, what have you, were not to be found. At least not for anyone larger than a ninety-eight-pound five-foot-tall ballerina. And God forbid I would ever lose that bra. Without getting too descriptive, if your school grades matched my cup size, you'd feed your report card to the family dog.

—Joan Churchill, "The Importance of Packing"

LAURIE GOUGH

The Summer of the Lost Ham

Hey, what happened to our stuff?

WE WEREN'T THE ONLY CANOEISTS PADDLING DOWN THE Yukon River that summer. About a dozen people were paddling along the same route at the same time. We all had our own pace and stopped at different times, but two or three times a day, we'd come across the same people, especially at campsites which were usually abandoned miners' camps or old Indian sites. We got to know our fellow river people, even fairly well sometimes, all of us part of a friendly assemblage of people of different ages, different countries and lifestyles but all encountering the same scenery, the same rain and sunshine, the same moose, and all with the same whimsical compulsion to paddle the Yukon River.

Even though we were in Canada, my friend and I were among the few Canadians on the river. Most of the other canoeists were German, Swiss, or American. Every day we'd pass the same spiky-hair Germans, two guys with leather jackets, tattoos, and lots of metal bits protruding from their flesh. They were usually fishing, which seemed incongruous.

Another pair of Germans we saw just once because they were hell-bent on making it to Dawson City as fast as possible. Since it was twenty-four-hour daylight, they refused to waste light and were paddling around the clock. There were six women from Florida that we came across at least three times a day. They were in their early fifties, on a college reunion, and this was their first canoe trip. Every time we met up with them they were laughing at a minor catastrophe they were either entering or escaping, and always the one named Marge was the butt of their jokes, since she insisted on applying make-up and styling her hair. "Mr. Right could be out here, honey, any time, around the corner," she told me. "You just don't know!"

The Albertan Brothers was the name we gave to two bald, not terribly bright twins from Alberta, each with his own canoe equipped with a small outboard motor. Often the Albertan Brothers would come ashore at a campsite for the "night" and cook dinner just as Kevin and I would be eating breakfast and preparing to set off for the "day." The twenty-four-hour daylight was confusing. We'd wake not knowing if it was 7 A.M. or 7 P.M. As time passed, I kept waiting for it to get dark. I felt as if I was missing something essential as each day continued on into the next without the familiar dream time to replenish what the day took away. The Albertan Brothers would never fail to ask us what time it was whenever we saw them. We never did know the time and I never understood why it was so important to them. "Does it really matter?" I finally said to them one morning, which was "one evening," for them. They had no reply but looked at me as if I'd told them I was holding secret meetings with the Pope deep inside the earth.

One morning as we paddled down the river we heard a voice shouting wildly. We looked up high to the top of a metal lookout tower beside the river, and there we found the voice's owner in the form of a giant man yelling at us. Dressed in army fatigues, he was nearly hysterical, waving his arms frantically. Incoherent and panic-stricken, he seemed to want desperately to tell us something. When we asked him if he wanted us to pull in, he shouted down, "Well, if y'all can, I'd mighty appreciate it."

We pulled in for him. He wasn't halfway down the tower when he started telling his tale, how he and his partner, hunters from Georgia, had capsized their canoe the day before in some monstrous rapids not far ahead, how he'd swum to shore and walked hours back along the riverbank to the tower he remembered passing, while his partner, who he thought was now probably dead, had stayed floating in the river to chase after the canoe, and save the ham. The lost case of beer was O.K. His wife was always nagging him to cut down anyway, but that mother of a honey-baked ham brought all the way from Georgia, they'd really been hankering after that. All that food, all that beer in the bottom of the river. It was a crying shame.

Ernie plunked himself down in the middle of our canoe, causing it to sink so deeply into the water I feared a river disaster myself. Out of breath, Ernie commenced a one-hour monologue. "Those rapids are a-comin soon and I ain't gonna fall out again. I'm gonna hang on. My wife. I gotta call my wife. I almost died yesterday and do ya think she cares? Probably not. I'm callin' her as soon as we get to a phone. We lost our ham, we lost our beer, shouldn't have been sittin' up on that beer case. Too shaky. Better to sit down low like this here. What part of the States you two from?" (The Canadian part, we told him.) "Hell, I gotta find my partner. I doubt he's alive."

Shortly afterwards we reached *the rapids* where the southern duo met their fate. The rapids were nothing more than a few barely discernable ripples in the water. How they'd managed to paddle through Lake Lebarge before this I couldn't fathom. "It ain't what she looks like. She's a trickster this river. Hang on." We paddled along as always, waiting for something terrible to happen. "O.K., maybe this is a better canoe. Those rapids were powerful yesterday. Nearly killed us. Jimmy, my partner, he's probably dead. Yep, won't be shootin' ducks with Jimbo no more."

Not far after the nonexistent rapids we came across Jimbo but Jimbo wasn't dead. He was relaxing with his face aimed into the sun beside a campfire he'd built. Next to him sat a sleeping pad propped on its side with the word HELP written across it in large letters. "Howdy all," Jimmy said, with a casual wave of his hand as if this were a church picnic. "Thought you'd be showin' up soon, Ern." Jimmy, in contrast to paunchy Ernie, was long and lean, slow-talking, with a scraggly red beard and felt hat pulled low over his head.

We pulled ashore. Ernie hauled his massive body out of the canoe, walked up to Jimmy, grabbed hold of him, and pulled rigid Jimmy into the wide spread of his sweaty chest, displaying a degree of tenderness I found surprising from this man who'd lamented his beer and his honey-baked Georgia ham. Jimmy, looking vaguely bewildered, didn't hug Ernie back but Ernie didn't seem to notice. "We ain't dead, Jimmy, we ain't dead. I love you, man. I love you... Where the hell's our canoe?"

"Gone."

"Ham?"

"Gone"

"Where's everything else?"

"Gone."

"How'd you get this fire lit? How'd you get this here sleepin' pad?"

"Some friendly folk come by. They helped a bit. They left."

That's when it struck me for the first time. Kevin and I may have to take Ernie and Jimmy with us for the rest of our canoe trip. I looked over at Kevin and could see the same thought was occurring dreadfully to him. A silent shudder passed between us.

But then, miraculously, we were saved. From around the bend the Albertan Brothers were approaching, each with his own canoe, even outboard motors, which would help lug the extra weight of Ernie. "Come ashore," we called to them. "Have some lunch."

At first the Albertan Brothers were happy to take along Ernie and Jimmy. Apparently the twins had been fighting, sick of each other's company, and were thankful for the distraction. But later that day, when they finally came across the Americans' upside-down canoe caught in a mass of dead trees near the shore, the Albertan Brothers were no longer on speaking terms with Ernie. We spotted Ernie and Jimmy ahead of us on the riverbank with their canoe, Ernie jumping up and down and waving at us, Jimmy lying on the ground, the pair of them stranded once again, at the mercy of whoever came down the river. Their canoe badly needed patching and the Albertan Brothers had unceremoniously dumped them there with it and left. "Stupid rednecks," said Ernie. "Trying to tell us everything we done wrong yesterday. As if they're any smarter." Since we didn't have room for the two of them, or any patches for their canoe, we were of no use to them and free to leave.

That night, at a campsite called Big Salmon, we learned that the six women from Florida had rescued Ernie and

Jimmy. Marge was beaming at the campfire, her rouged cheeks flaming, her coifed hair all astray. Jimmy, pulling on his beard and stealing quick shy glances her way, was a changed man, a man whose last name apparently was Right. Marge and Jimmy had fallen in love.

And so it went, the Yukon River, inspiring love and languor and a never-ending light. In the day we floated and at night we recalled, trying to rehearse the scenes of the river in our minds: the eagles and the leggy moose, the impossible green of the river and the mountains rising up so close like sudden thoughts. The nights too never failed to bring with them, on schedule and at a distinct required decibel level, the not-too-distant voice of Ernie telling his story of the river disaster which almost took his life, the story of how he'd been so close to death he'd spoken to God and asked forgiveness—forgiveness for what we never asked—how he'd swum miles alone along the river, searching for his partner, a tale of heroic proportions we didn't even recognize, a tale Kevin and I, by its fifth telling, had been cut out of entirely. "I don't understand," said a Swiss man to me one night around a campfire. "Every night we hear this same story and every night the story grows more dangerous." The Swiss man told us he also had canoed by the hysterical Ernie in the tower, but hadn't stopped for him. He simply waved and kept paddling, thinking Ernie in his army fatigues must be an escaped lunatic from the military. "This sometimes happens in Switzerland. The army drives them mad and they head for the wilderness. I didn't want to go near him."

On the tenth day we looked up from the river to see a bridge approaching. The bridge seemed intrusive and alien and meant civilization was ahead. A few minutes later we passed some shacks along the water and a clearing of the forest. Sadly, we'd arrived at Carmacks and the end of our canoe trip. Carmacks was a forgettable little town with three restaurants all owned by the same man, which explained our ten-dollar salad consisting solely of iceberg lettuce.

That night, camping in our tent beside a river that felt like home, I thought of the drifters, homesteaders, and renegades who had tramped across an unimaginable expanse of country and sailed down a river to find gold, or their spirits, or a new life. I thought of the ones who died on the way, their bones left at the river's bottom, polished, and fragile. You could almost hear their voices, a murmur around your sleep, as if the dead souls were babbling at the edge of the river. And I thought of Ernie, whose bones the river didn't want, and whose babbling at the edge of the river was enough to waken the dead.

Laurie Gough is the author of Kite Strings of the Southern Cross, *which won a silver medal for Foreword Magazine's Best Travel Book of the Year, and was short-listed for the Thomas Cook/Daily Telegraph Travel Book of the Year award in the U.K. She has also written for Salon.com,* Outpost, *and the* Toronto Globe and Mail. *Her work appears in several travel anthologies, including* Travelers' Tales: A Woman's World, The Adventure of Food, Greece, Her Fork in the Road, *and* Wanderlust: Real-Life Tales of Adventure and Romance. *She lives in Ontario, Canada.*

LORI MAYFIELD

Scared Shitless on Safari

True friendship can survive almost anything.

HEAVY SIGHS FILLED WITH TERRORIZED ANGST WOKE ME from a dead sleep. Wrung out at the edge of her cot was the silhouette of my best friend and worst-matched travel companion, Beth. "Do you hear the lions?" she quivered.

Yes, off in the distance, I could hear throaty growls punctuated with a yawn-like roar, but I'd dismissed it as hairball clearings.

"They're probably just marking their territory, Beth. Go back to sleep."

"I have to go to the bathroom *so* bad," she pleaded.

Unlike Abercrombie & Fitch, which strung electric fencing around their camps, Wilderness Travel simply hired a local night watchman armed with a spear.

"Shine your flashlight outside the tent opening so the Masai guard will come over and walk you to the toilet tent," I suggested.

"And have the lion rip my arm off!" Beth snapped. She'd been afraid of everything on our African adventure to date including fear of the airplane crash-landing in Johannesburg, someone breaking into our hotel room in Nairobi and being swallowed by the river, camping along the Ewaso-Ngiro in the Sambura National Reserve. Tonight only marked the next item up for neurotic meltdown.

"Do you want me to walk over there with you?" I offered.

"No." Beth began to sob.

"What do you want me to do?" I said, annoyed.

"Would you mind if I peed in the tent?" she begged.

"Are you serious? Where?"

"I'll go in my water bottle."

"How are you going to whiz in a half-inch opening?" I asked, trying to drum some sense into her.

Relieved that I was open to even discussing the idea, Beth explained. "I can dump the water out, cut the top off with my Swiss army knife, pee, then toss the bottle out of the tent." Clearly she'd been awake longer than I thought devising such a scheme.

Interpreting my stunned silence as a green light, I could already hear the sound of plastic being cut with tiny scissors, a rustling around at the edge of Beth's cot and a stream of urine hitting the empty plastic bottle that seemed to flow and flow and flow. I rolled over in my cot to try and go back to sleep.

"Goddamn it!" Beth announced.

"Did you miss?" I asked.

"No, I have diarrhea."

My eyes opened wide.

"Would you mind if I…"

Bolting upright I said, "You are not diarrheaing in this tent!" I marched over and unzipped the front of the tent. "If you stink in here, you'll lure one of those lions over here to eat us both."

Pajama pants at her ankles, holding a half liter of pee, Beth was sacrificed to the lions. Crawling back into my sunken cot, I tried to get back to sleep, only to be roused a few minutes later by the zip of the tent opening.

"Did the Masai guy walk you to the toilet tent?" I asked, astonished at how quickly she'd returned.

"No," Beth said sheepishly. "I went in front of our tent."

"You think a lion's not going catch a whiff of that and come kill whatever left that god-awful stench?"

Beth chuckled and went right to sleep.

Listening to her snore, I lay wide-awake wondering how far away the lions really were.

The next hour I wondered what might provoke a lion to become man-eating. If say, a lion accidentally stepped in a pile of human dung, could that be enough to set it off?

The hour after that I wondered if Beth even bothered to kick any dust over her territory-marking, given that she was in her bare feet.

And the hour after that I didn't have to wonder anymore as it was now morning and I heard the six-year old from the family camping next to us scream, "Mom, look! Grrr-oss!"

Lori Mayfield has averted lions in travels since to India, Nepal, Costa Rica, the Turks and Caicos Islands, and she is currently getting over jetlag from Vietnam. She funds her travels as a freelance advertising copywriter in Los Angeles, only recently embarking into the world of travel writing. Her tales of travel have also appeared in The Los Angeles Times.

MARGO KAUFMAN

No Crater Love

Never tell a woman what she can't do.

IT'S AMAZING THE CRAZY THINGS YOU DO ON VACATION. Duke woke me up before dawn. "It's time to climb the volcano," he said. I could hear the little voices pleading: "Stay in the hotel. Get a cold drink. Relax. Read a book." But I didn't want to miss The Experience.

We were on a small island in east Indonesia called Bandanaira, the fulfillment of my husband's yen to get off the beaten track. There are five cars on the island, no phones, no hot water, and no innerspring mattresses. Across the lagoon, we could see Gunung Api, another tropical island, whose only amenity is a picturesque volcano, complete with fresh lava and a plume of smoke.

One night we saw a film of the 1988 eruption. Highlights included a mushroom cloud, rivers of molten lava running into the sea, and a mass evacuation to the nearest safe refuge—150 miles away. This was unsettling enough, but then the owner of our hotel asked, "Who wants to climb Gunung Api?" Anyone who makes it becomes an honorary citizen.

I had no desire to risk my life to become a member of a primitive island whose hazards included not only volcanism but typhoons, tidal waves, earthquakes, and, until recently, slave insurrections. But Duke thought that it would be "fun" to get a view. I should have let him go without me.

I would have let him go without me. But then he uttered those fatal words: "You can't do it, honey. It's too hard." Immediately, my ego went into overdrive. There was no way I was going to let him be the star of our vacation slides.

The speedboat landed on the shores of Gunung Api at five-thirty A.M. Even though I've never had a positive experience at that hour in my life, I was optimistic. Three other guests were making the climb, along with two guides. I was relieved to see Martine, a cheerful Australian chain-smoker in penny loafers. "If she can do it, I can do it," I confidently told Duke.

I got a little nervous when her eighteen-year-old brother, Luke, turned out to be a mountain racer who was going for the speed record. He bounded into the thicket like a deer. Then, to my dismay, Martine ground out her cigarette and loped out of view. "She's only twenty-three," Duke reminded me.

Still, I didn't worry until I realized that I was in for a 2,198-foot straight vertical ascent (666 meters, the number of the devil in the Bible, appropriately enough). There were no switchbacks, no convenient shoulders with gradual slopes, not even a clearly marked trail. The air temperature was 85 degrees and rising. Humidity: 95 percent.

Bruce, a soft-spoken third-grade teacher transplanted from Santa Rosa to Java and the winner of the Thirty-Something Sensitive Guy Sweepstakes, suggested that I lead what was left of the pack. "Just set your own pace," he said reassuringly as

I crawled along on all fours, clinging to vegetation that I prayed wouldn't be uprooted. Branches whipped back and lashed my face as I desperately struggled to avoid the three sizes of loose rocks: the small ones that got into my shoes, the medium ones that bounced off my ankles, and the large ones, which threatened to snap off my ankle.

"You're doing fine," Bruce said.

"You're never going to make it," said Duke, barely fifteen minutes into the climb. "I'll take you back." I didn't want to give him the satisfaction. But I didn't want to die either.

"Remember the story about the Little Engine That Could?" Bruce said. "'I think I can. I think I can.'"

> The main difference between men and women is that men are lunatics and women are idiots.
>
> —Rebecca West

I didn't think *I* could, but suddenly Alden, the friendly Bandanese guide in the traditional Bandu mountain footwear—bright yellow flip-flops—scurried ahead of me and gave me a hand. With his help, I began to make steady progress.

"I'll get you a gold volcano if you get to the top," Duke said.

I got to the top. Luke was there, smiling triumphantly. He'd set a new record: forty-eight minutes. Martine was enjoying a cigarette. Me, I inhaled the reeking volcanic acids. I saw sulfur blooms on hot rocks. I felt no joy, wonder, or pride, only a keen sense of imminent danger. "And *you* missed the five-hundred-foot sheer drop into the caldera," said Duke, who'd viewed it precariously from the unstable lip.

I wish I'd missed the trip down, which was even more treacherous than the ascent. One false step would bring a three-hundred-foot slide into a thorn bush—if you were lucky. When the ordeal was finally over, I embraced my mate. "Thanks for not saying 'I told you so,'" I said.

"Thanks for helping me save face," Duke said. "If I'd had to keep up with Luke, I'd be in intensive care." Duke then suggested that we spend the rest of the day lying motionless on a secluded beach.

It's amazing the crazy things you do on vacation.

Margo Kaufman's work has appeared in The New York Times, The Los Angeles Times Magazine, Cosmopolitan, USA Today, The Village Voice, *and she is the Hollywood correspondent for* Pug Talk *magazine. She is the author of three books, including* 1-800-Am-I-Nuts, *from which this story was excerpted and she lives in Venice, California, with her husband and two pugs.*

⁂

It is raining when our plane touches down. I look through the double airplane window, wondering how bugs get trapped between the two panes, and I see that it is raining and I know I've made a colossal mistake, an epic mistake. There is a strange man sitting beside me and he is holding my hand. I have no idea who this man is; what is he trying to do? *Comfort* me? And although I can clearly recall that yesterday following a brief proclamation from a rabbi, I had agreed to spend the rest of my life with this hand holder, that is hardly reason to trust him with my life.

I am sure every woman at one moment or another tells some version of this—the husband-cum-stranger bit. It's a bonding ritual between us, as satisfyingly anecdotal as the locker-room brag. Perhaps more so: I didn't just fuck him, I *married* him. But then, oh shit. Newlywed reality is a plane ride to a foreign land and the person sitting next to you is not your mother.

—Cynthia Kaplan, *Why I'm Like This: True Stories*

MICHELE PETERSON

* * *

Hat Head

There's a reason we take souvenir photos.

"JUNE 6, 2002 (RUETERS) HONG KONG WOMAN LOSES lawsuit for compensation against hair salon which she claimed made her look like Osama bin Laden when she wanted a hairstyle like Hollywood actress Julia Roberts."

I know exactly how she must have felt. I always feel that way shortly after friends begin to flip politely through my carefully assembled scrapbook entitled "Hong Kong—1997." I can see the inevitable question begin to form and, just when they can't hold it in any longer, it escapes, "Wow, what was with the hair?" Once the question is out in the open, they are liberated from social convention and flip faster and faster through whirling pages in search of even more fantastic examples of the failure of modern hair-styling products. "Bad Hair" days. We all have them. Flyaway hair, fright hair, bush head, and all their variations should be considered a travel advisory. They have the power to destroy more good photo shots than any other travel peril, and here's the proof:

My trip to Hong Kong had begun rather innocently with

an invitation from my sister to meet her there. I left the planning to her as I was busy in the corporate world and she was the acknowledged expert in all things Asian. In fact, as a member of the Jackie Chan fan club she even had a photo of herself, arms wrapped around him, to prove it. As it turned out, everything she learned was from old martial arts movies and our holiday was an adventure in very bad hair—namely mine.

One clear spring day I received a hefty package in the mail. It contained a lot of information about our destination and a handwritten note from my sister which said that she was off to get her hair trimmed in anticipation of the humidity. I didn't read the material but followed suit on the haircut and, in a demonstration of my enthusiasm and commitment, went even further than a trim and nodded "yes" to a "summer cut." While innocuous-looking at first, much like the large broccoli-shaped plants unleashed by the meteor shower in the sci-fi thriller, *The Day of the Triffids*, my haircut would soon begin mutations of its own and would travel the world, horrifying those it encountered along the way.

I survived the transpacific flight with only slightly flattened hair but was feeling pretty light-headed when we landed. A computer glitch had recorded my dietary preference as "fruiterian" and I didn't need an explanation about what that meant when I saw that my snack was a package of dried cranberries and lunch was a giant fruit plate complemented by a fruit bun and jam and all the juice I could swallow.

The jet's steep descent over the harbor, past towering black skyscrapers and finally into the old airport in Kowloon, exhilarated and then quickly faded from memory once I arrived at our guest house. Wondering why the front desk personnel averted their eyes when I picked up the key, one look in the mirror was enough to provide shocking evidence of the damage humidity and the wind of a midnight taxi race could do to my hair. It was basically a round ball á la Don King, except I'm not black or famous. To my sister's credit, she didn't say a word. But then again, she couldn't. As it turned out, the heat and humidity was so intense that in desperation she had showered and lain down stark naked on the bed to cool off. Unfortunately, our elderly host took that moment to fling open the door to show the room to a prospective investor. We'll never know if he made the investment but the vision before him was no doubt imprinted in his memory forever.

That night, before we retired, my sister set out her Pandora's box of survival supplies for my appreciation and I noted a carton of fifty plastic forks, some Triscuits, and what appeared to be a can of Bavarian mini-wieners, before I drifted off.

The next day, we headed out, a little later than planned, to take the Kowloon–Canton railway to the Ten Thousand Buddhas Temple. I'd needed the extra time to crouch before a mirror, hung no more than two feet above the floor, to try to tame the twisting tendrils of my determined hair. Once enroute and after a short ride, we were sure we could see one of the Bountiful Buddhas through the foliage, so we hopped off. Our luck continued when we spotted a taxi cab waiting patiently by the curb. We jumped in and with a cry of "Ten Thousand Buddhas" expected to take off in haste. Instead, he shouted "No Buddha" and our attempts to correct our instructions to "Big Buddha" and "Bountiful Buddha" just made him angrier.

No matter, as we could now see a bronze Buddha high up

around the corner. Commending our honest driver for his reluctance to bilk us for such a short fare, we headed out on foot. My opinion of my sister rose quickly when she snapped open an umbrella to offer shade from the beating sun and quickly melted into the crowd climbing the hundreds of stairs which lay ahead. I was less fortunate and burned my ears, neck, and scalp on the ascent but I was sure that I could hear the crickets singing as promised as we neared the peak. We took a few shots on the way up and my photo album records the awful evidence—the bangs of my hair, spread to a wing span of immense proportions, the curl mirroring the slope of the distant pagoda roofs in perfect symmetry. I appeared to have developed some sort of weird, Asian version of a traditional little Dutch girl's hat—except I couldn't take mine off.

> Mirror, Mirror,
> On the Wall,
> I Don't Want to Hear
> One Word Out of You.
>
> —Jean Kerr

At the top of the hill there were plenty of Buddhas. But as we toured one small temple after another it became apparent that these were not the Buddhas of antiquity, each expressive and donated by thousands of grateful worshippers over the years. Rather, these were disposable plastic replicas interspersed with M&M's and photos of family relatives. We were at the Asian equivalent of a Rest Haven—a mausoleum. And those weren't tour guides circling but salespeople. My sister and I quickly assumed expressions signifying satisfaction with the homage we had performed for our distant ancestors and made a beeline back down the hill. We passed our driver who was still resting in his taxi and sped back by train to the city.

The next day, we took the same train. Without even being asked, my sister had walked to the store to purchase a gel product described as "The most efficient product for keeping your hair steadily in place." With confidence, I had liberally applied it before departing for the day. Our destination this time was the New Territories, the long-disputed border to China, and we intended to stay on the train long enough to enjoy the promised pleasures of expanses of rice paddies, bamboo groves, and fields of singing birds. We were just past the sprawling concrete suburbs of apartment complexes and I could almost hear the birds singing when the conductor boarded our car and waved everyone off with a shout. There was no mistaking the intent so we followed the throng and exited—surely two stops short of China.

Once inside the terminal, we appeared to be inside a huge mall designed as in nowhere else but Asia. It was a rabbit warren of hundreds of narrow shops selling Hello Kitty stationery, porcelain teapots, and herbal remedies. But we were in luck, this was dim sum restaurant heaven and in one bright establishment, with seating for close to a thousand, we found a vacant table easily. There were no menus but things looked promising when tea was delivered without even asking. The dim sum delivery ladies snaked in a long line among the tables shouting out their offerings. All around us diners munched on shrimp balls and tiny fragrant delicacies. My sister waved down the nearest lady and pointed with confidence to the top basket. We each received a glutinous dollop in our bowls and the first recorded scribble was made on our menu card. More dollops and scribbles followed and we were no closer to finding anything that didn't quiver. In fact, I think that word spread and soon every purveyor of wobbly goods was bearing down on our table. I think they were paid by commission, as they were soon lined up hoping to fulfill our every jiggling-food fantasy. The one bonus was that my ever-prepared sister did not have to dig into her stash of plastic forks as we could simply slurp up whatever was placed in front of us.

Dizzy now, we headed back to the train and peered out the window at the now-diminishing Chinese border. My gaze locked on my reflection and in horror I saw that the MSG in our meal had caused a reaction worthy of note in the oddities of Ripley's Believe It or Not. My lips had tripled in size and severe welts circled my face but they paled beside the crowning glory of my hair. Like an overinflated shower cap, it rose in a strange mushroom-like form, an alien entity hovering above.

Over the next several days, I fought for hair mastery with a product that promised "It will cement your hairstyle for many hours, even in the course of heavy winds." Although I never did find a wind strong enough to take the challenge, the super gel did have an unexpected benefit. For some time, I had wondered why every corner store sold mentholated Kleenex but soon learned by observation that relief from the smog could be found by fashioning a face mask from the tissues. Bad days required several while a light day needed only a single. I took pride that, thanks to my new super gel, barely one elastic band was needed to attach my makeshift smog protector securely.

Needing an escape from the smog, I caught the Star Ferry very early one morning and crossed to Hong Kong island. From there it was an hour's ride across the South China Sea and into Mui Wo where Silvermine Bay juts into Lantau

Island. There would be no missing the Big Buddha this time as I knew that it was 35 meters high, 250 tons of gleaming bronze, and accessible by bus down one long road. I caught the bus without incident as it was conveniently labeled "Big Buddha." Even at the early hour, it was already half full with women laughing and braiding each other's long dark hair. The ocean spray on the ferry ride had given my hair one final metamorphosis. Light and full, it billowed around me like a dandelion seed puff. I considered asking one of the women to show mercy and braid my hair too but, instead, used some of the precious water from my flask to paste it all down as best I could. It was clearly winning the battle.

I gazed out the window at the scenery weaving by. Wisps of a moonlike mist rose off the fields as our bus climbed the green hills and rolled past stands of thin bamboo that rustled in the breeze. Sounds of temple bells caught the wind, armloads of incense jutted from sand inside urns, billowing their choking sweet perfume and monks in flowing orange robes glided by open doorways as we alighted from the bus. My companions scattered.

Much later, Buddha found, I wandered by the nearby fishing village of Tai-O. Its ramshackle houses were perched on stilts, lining the river that supported the village life. A sampan neared and a woman much older than I stood, capably steering her narrow craft through the boats and household debris that lined the docks. With recognition, we saw that we wore matching hats. Days earlier, I had laughed, beyond control, when my sister had strolled the resort island of Cheung Chau wearing the identical hat, but then I picked one up myself. I had never seen a piece of apparel that more closely resembled a fried egg with its impossibly wide brim, barely rounded yolk crown, and shade circumference of over three feet.

Today, I saw my reflection across the wide river channel and across a broad cultural gap and my crazy hair no longer mattered. As the sampan lady passed, we lifted our hats off to each other, tipping them to our differences and our similarities and smiled.

Michele Peterson is a freelance writer and business executive who always travels with a hat—just in case.

E. JEAN CARROLL

Women Who Run with No Clothes On

Following the lead of ecofeminists, she finds her inner Cornish game hen.

HERE WE ARE IN THE SWEAT LODGE. IT'S THE FIRST NIGHT of the trip. Shhhh—no casual talk here. The sweat lodge is a big blue plastic tarp wrapped around three oars. You sweat like a yak in the sweat lodge! Some sisters are not welcome here. Their energy is not good because they have the curse. They have to sit in the moon lodge. Pam and Robin are in the moon lodge.

The rest of us are passing the ladle and pouring Colorado River water on heated rocks. Pam and Robin are in the moon lodge eating three pounds of peanut M&M's. Man! Look at that steam—I can't see anything else. River, the Miss Manners of the sweat lodge, is beating her drum. Pam and Robin are in the moon lodge (Robin's tent), probably listening to Pearl Jam on a portable tape player. We are shaking our rattles. We made them out of gourds. They were "specially grown for us by Margaret," whoever that is. I'm feeling a little faint. Oh! A sister just passed me the lemonade. "All my relations." That's what you say. "All my relations."

UUUUUUEEEEEEK! Well, I just drank a mug of filthy Colorado River water. Now we are howling our wolf calls. Honey, are you sure American Indians did this?

Well, have you ever seen an American Indian with really fabulous skin?

We are about fifty miles downstream from Moab, Utah, on the Colorado River, which is roaring by at about 19,000 cubic feet per second.

In the old days, instead of saying cubic feet per second, we just said, "The river killed two people last week." Those were the days when going on a "woman's trip" meant you were driving downtown to buy stencils to redecorate the kitchen.

Now it means that sixteen of my wolf-sisters and I are heading down ninety-six miles of Colorado River, the whole trip being "facilitated" by the celebrated priestess and acupuncturist River and guided by Sheri Griffith, a former rodeo queen, owner of the world's largest woman-run adventure company, and an equal-opportunity employer—she occasionally requires her male guides to wear skirts. ("A nice one, elastic waistband. They don't work otherwise.") Needless to say, there are none of that sex on this trip.

> Does it seem sometimes that the world is out to destroy our self-esteem? Avoid, at all costs, any company that makes you feel worse about yourself. For example, those commuter airlines with a box at the ticket check-in that says "If your hips won't fit in here, you're too big for our ride." That's just rude!
>
> —Leigh Anne Jasheway, *I'm Not Getting Older (I'm Getting Better At Denial)*

Ecofeminism is such a trend! And across the nation this powerful force has been coupled with the fad for *Women Who Run with the Wolves*, the colossal bestseller of a few years ago written by Clarissa Pinkola Estes, Ph.D., which tells stories about goddesses, witches, enchantresses, and hags and generally whips the female sex into such frenzies that they forsake their houses and run wild in the streets like packs of dingoes. And when you throw in a *soigné* float down a big river with seventeen women who have not only snapped their leashes but are also learning to "see through their nipples" like Baubo the goddess, what you've got is a Class V postfeminist version of Revo Dames meets Greenpeace.

About nine o'clock the next morning and we're loading the J-rig and the eighteen-foot oar-boat when Terry, a social worker who specializes in drug addicts, returns from the toilet.

"I was out there having my morning coffee," she says excitedly. "So I walked back there…I left my coffee here…and I walked…and in the pee bucket was a chipmunk. Drowning!"

"Oh, no!" says Hanto Yo!.

"He was on his last legs," says Terry. "He was like this!"

She rolls her eyes up in her head.

"God!" exclaims Hanta Yo!, nervously adjusting her hydrating neckerchief.

"He couldn't get out," says Terry. Terry is wearing a cerise tank top and an Annie Lennox hairdo with an attractive neck fringe and is from Bayonne, New Jersey, and consequently sounds like an elegant cross between Bruce Springsteen and a dugong in estrus. "And I said, 'Oh, my God!' So I bent the can over a little, and I stuck my hand in. And into my hand he walked!"

Hanta Yo! stands a moment in shocked contemplation, her cowboy hat tipped back on her head.

"In my hand," says Terry, dropping her voice tenderly. The night before, in the sweat lodge, she had sent a prayer to the spirits to save her sister, who is suffering from cancer. "I put him on the rock and I petted his back, and he was shaking so much because he was so frightened. And I petted him and petted him, and he got up and he ran a little and then he ran a little more, and then he ran away."

You've already run with the wolves. You've run away from the wolves. Heck, you've even cleaned up after the wolves. Why not just sit back and howl at the moon for a while?

—Leigh Anne Jasheway, *I'm Not Getting Older (I'm Getting Better At Denial)*

Hanta Yo! pats Terry joyfully on the back. Hanta Yo! has a Billy Idol flattop and a green tank top that says WORK SUCKS, I'M GOING TO THE RIVER. Back in Glendale, California, where she has just retired after twenty-seven years as a probation officer, Hanta Yo! is known as Sandy. Hanta Yo! is her river name. It means "Clear the way!" in the Sioux language. River, our priestess, has suggested that we all take river names. Hanta Yo! has a cigarette between her fingers and a copy of *Women Who Run with the Wolves* under her arm.

"I wish we had an Indian name for a woman who saves chipmunks," says Hanta Yo! thoughtfully.

"My river name is going to be Chipmunk!" says Terry.

Hanta Yo! frowns and looks down at the sand in concentration.

"I wish I knew the name for a woman named Chipmunk

who saves chipmunks," she says, smiling and shrugging her shoulders.

Good. Fine. Here is where the action should start. First a little whitewater, and then—*boom!*—women so frightened, and vomiting so hard, that they pass through Satan's Gut completely unconscious. That's the manly formula. Right into the Good Stuff. That's the way they do it, I know, I know. But look what we've got. Already thirty miles downstream and still nothing but that sweat lodge. Worse, the Colorado is wide and deep for another twenty miles, and my wolf-sisters have slathered themselves in glitter oil and are sprawled half-naked over the rafts like plump young tarts in a James Bond movie, drinking beer, eating apples, and yodeling off the canyon walls. I, of course, have every inch of my body covered with SPF 30 protective clothing, black spandex, and a 3X beaver.

The J-rig is a big old twenty-five-foot-long baby-blue pontoon boat with three fat tubes jutting off the front, a thirty-horse Mariner outboard on the back ("We are pro-choice," says Sheri about the prop), and Molly's canary yellow Zambezi oar-boat lashed to its side (to be detached in the rapids, of course). We have all brought so much stuff we look like a big squid floating down the river covered with barnacles.

River, our priestess, has blessed both boats, naturally, and smudged them. *What?* You don't know what smudging is? You don't know what River means when she says, "We're going to be traveling into other realities on this trip," and lights up a pile of grass in a seashell and holds it under your nose, swelling your nostrils to the size of Brussels sprouts?

"The power of the smoke takes us to the spirit world," says River, who has studied Chinese, Native American, and naturopathic medicines, plus gone to medical school; who is wearing purple-and-aquamarine spirit braids with tiny silver drums and long feather earrings; and who begins fanning the smoke against your neck, then across your shoulders, over your chest, your waist, and so on down to the bottoms of your feet. That is smudging. It "cleanses" the body for "the journey." River's smudge turns out to be made of cedar (for harmony), sage (for purifying), sweet grass (for sweetness), and juniper sap (because, says River, "it's got a kick-ass smell").

We smudge one another from eyelids to ankles so often it's like a two-pack-a-day habit. The scent of juniper sap is clinging to our hair. Good God! What a boatload of smudgers we are! We also do a little breathing in the warrior stance and, on a multitude of occasions, shake our gourds. Robin, a tiny, chocolate-gobbling, Coke-swigging, baggy-shorts-wearing, Dorothy-Parker-talking, green-eyed blonde from Tennessee who works with troubled adolescents, was in her tent drinking a can of Hershey's syrup when we did the gourds, so she just shakes her complimentary Sheri Griffith insulated drinking cup, which she has filled with rocks.

Sometimes, when we're floating down the water, River reads aloud to us from *Women Who Run with the Wolves* about Baubo, who "talks through her vulva" and "sees through her nipples." Other times, she reads from a book "written by a stone."

We float by canyons where scenes from *Thelma and Louise* were shot and eat bags of potato chips. "What's Richard Cranium's nickname?" says Charnel, an artist who works with cow skulls and is now into metal and has made a six-foot-tall copper corn plant with two turquoise kernels.

"Dick Head!" we shout.

The first two mornings we cry. "Oh! Hail, O mighty river goddess! May our passage be safe!" When we arrive at a beach for lunch, Hanta Yo!, who eats like a wild hyena, is the first one off the raft. When we leave, Sheri reminds us to "dip" before we get in the boat.

"What for?" says River, who threw off most of her clothes yesterday and never put them back on again. "Some women may *want* sand in their crotch."

It is 125 degrees in the sun and another 125 degrees in the sand. That makes 250 degrees. Any other group of women would have hurled themselves into the river and refused to budge. Not these women. Only the second day of the trip, and they are going to hike straight up a mesa to see a thousand-year-old ruin from the great Anasazi civilization. A torrent of boiling lava could roar down the canyon and these ladies, smudged from forehead to pubis with juniper sap, would crawl on toward the sacred spot.

At the top, it's a bit of a shock. Nobody's seen anything like it. The fat brown river is far, far below. A rising sun, several handprints, and a dainty antelope are painted on the mauve rock. And rolling out in front of us is an ochre ocean with big red whales blowing out under the bright blue sky. River, our priestess, squats in the dirt and rubs dust on her chest. It mixes glamorously with the glitter oil and gives her curvy, half-naked torso the rich amber shade of a Havana cigar. Lit.

We sit down near the noble Anasazi granary. No, that doesn't work. First Dolores, an American Indian who works with disabled children, smudges us, and then we sit down, befuddled under the enormous load of the sun. It is so hot even the scorpions do not move. Despite the appalling temperature, Charnel drums like Phil Collins in a malarial fever. River shakes her bone rattle. Indeed, it would seem impossible that a human carcass could stand out in the direct rays wearing only a cowboy hat and a thong bottom and take us on a journey down a spiral staircase where we "hear the wind, feel a stone on the ground beneath our butts," and meet our mothers and grandmothers and great-grandmothers and all the women who have gone before us and shake our gourds at them and have them shake their gourds back at us, but River manages with spiritual aplomb.

O.K., O.K., O.K. Some women think it's a load of crap. Other women, Dodie in particular, who recently lost her mother, get something out of it, something straight, something like being a bird let out of a cage, or something like being on speaking terms with an angel. I don't know what I think. Next on the program is Dolores (Rhonda's river name), the *genuine* American Indian. Although at this point the sun has burned through our brains and is shining out our eyeballs, Dolores steps to the edge of the cliff, a marvel with waist-length black hair, a great wonder like the sand and the cactus flowers, like the rocks and the sun, like the river and the stars, and suddenly the air turns cooler as she sings to her ancestors in a voice so smooth and velvety it's like snow flurries blowing down from the Arctic.

Can you believe it? It's day three of this *river* trip, and honey, we are on another *hike*. This time it's up to a waterfall, everybody's scaling the rocks, running barefoot through the mosses and lichen, and oh, geez, they're stripping off their clothes again. Yes, they're throwing their clothes all over the rocks and running up, climbing, pulling each other up, laughing, to a grotto, splashing, squealing. Molly's rump is as red as a mandrill's from sliding down the rocks. Oh, no, girls! I'm not taking my clothes off. I'm from a *respectable* publication.

I'll throw myself off this cliff before I take my clothes off. This long-sleeved, double-pocketed, double-vented, crocus-yellow Ex Officio sun-resistant shirt, this Maidenform brassiere, these beige SPF 36 Frogwear trousers, these white cotton underpants, these knee socks, these tennis shoes, these leather driving gloves, and this Giorgio Armani felt hat with chin strap stay on.

No, ma'am! I once marched across Papua New Guinea and kept my skin so alabaster white that the entire population of a five-hut village near the border of Irian Jaya took me for a ghost.

No way, José. Even my ex-husbands never saw me from the rear, naked.

We are on the beach making drums at twilight. First we thank our cow for her hide—our cow, which "stood in the field in the night and in the day and in the snow and in the rain and lived and breathed, and was killed without a prayer." Normally I would have collapsed in the mud and sobbed like Oprah Winfrey on the "Barbara Walters Special" when River started thanking my cow. But I am a different woman.

None of my ex-husbands may have seen me from the rear naked, but I have now seen myself from the rear naked, like Narcissus in the mountain pool, and the sight of it peeled my eyeballs. It gave me the shock of my life. I'd never seen my own body till that moment. And my giggles woke me up. I was baptized in the name of Insouciance, Spunk, and

Madcap, amen. In fact, the girls had to drag me out of the water. And it's all thanks to this silly river trip. The further we retreat from Madison Avenue, the International Slaughterhouse of the Female Image, the deeper we travel down the river, the higher we climb into canyons, the more beautiful the bodies of the women become. Indeed, if I myself am not voted Miss Utah by the time we hit Lake Powell, I'll be surprised.

We have reached the confluence of the Green and Colorado rivers. Just past the confluence is a sign that says DANGER! CATARACT CANYON. HAZARDOUS RAPIDS.

Two weeks ago three people in a wooden speedboat went beyond this sign. The sign is high up on a cliff. Even if you miss the sign, you can feel the difference in the water. At this juncture the Colorado River almost doubles in cubic feet per second. They are still looking for two of the bodies.

We are sitting on shore, as composed as at a funeral. Usually Charnel would be saying, "What's cowboy foreplay?" and we'd be saying, "What?" and Charnel would be saying, "Get in the truck, bitch!" but today it's raining, and Gitta, who along with Molly is one of Sheri's star guides, is giving us a "little talk."

"Cataract Canyon is a pool-drop rapid canyon," says Gitta. Oh, you'd swear we were at Seneca Falls being addressed by Susan B. Anthony. "The rapids begin small but get progressively larger as the canyon constricts." Gitta rowed on the U.S. national championship team in college and is five feet, eleven inches tall and weighs 163 pounds.

Not even Big Shirley, who looks exactly like Rodin's statue of Balzac, is as big as Gitta. Gitta was born in Belgium; Big Shirley is a grandmother from Moab with a flask of Black

Velvet. She teaches English and won the trip in a raffle in support of Seekhaven, the domestic violence crisis center that Sheri helped found in Moab.

"Hand signals are important because in whitewater you can't hear anything," says Gitta. "This"—she pats the top of her head—"means 'I'm O.K.' So if you've been thrown out of the boat, we'll go like this"—she pats the top of her head again—"'Are you all right?'" Gitta is wearing a Sheri Griffith Expeditions cap with three eagle feathers dangling out the back and is so beautiful it's frightening. "And you respond"—she pats the top of her head. In whitewater Gitta wears a royal-blue sequin bustier in honor of the river goddess.

"Um, if you're not O.K., use this signal."

She makes a fist.

"What if you're unconscious?" I ask.

Uh-oh. Here comes Sheri. Walking across the shallows, her canvas hat hung with silver doodads, her gold-and-turquoise sarong tied low on one hip, her hot-pink sports bra shimmering in the gray light.

"I have a reputation," she says, pulling the cap off her lip balm, "that everybody comes back smiling" (smiling, and giving her mouth a swipe).

We are camping tonight at Little Upset rapids. Gitta and Molly are making Cornish game hens. We are lying on our backs in the sand in a circle with our drums and journeying to find our power animals. River's power animal is a white rattlesnake. River says whenever she takes her power animal on job interviews she always gets the position. Catherine, a quiet, gentle, big-bosomed, ladylike nurse, is lying on the ground with her drum, journeying for her power animal. She opens her eyes and sees a wolf. She and the wolf run swiftly, lightly, long-leggedly, smiling and laughing, at the pace of Jackie Joyner-Kersee in the 800 meters, up and down the beach together on the edge of the water. When Catherine tells River she's running up and down the beach with the wolf, River cries because Catherine has a disability that sometimes makes even walking difficult.

I don't know what my power animal is, but I think it could be a Cornish game hen.

We are on the J-rig and you can see the rapids ahead. I am looking for the top to my number-45 sunscreen and taking my notebook out of its plastic sandwich bag and trying to remember what I wanted to jot down about the excitement of seeing the rapids, and suddenly I hear Dolores saying, "We're not in Kansas anymore." I glance up and every follicle of my body stands on end. A wall of water has rolled up directly in front of the boat. In the half-second before it hits—as I am thinking, "Somebody is going to owe me a lot of money," and my heart suddenly attains absolute maximum expansion—I see behind it a bigger wall of water, and then the first wall crashes over our heads. Never in my life, not even looking at my own rear two days ago, never, never, never—the boat is climbing, impossibly climbing, you think you're never going to get to the top and then you get to the top and absolutely nothing happens, you are standing utterly still, and well, you go completely out of your head. You are riding so far on The Edge, your fear turns into ecstasy. You can't help yourself. You begin screaming gibberish. You howl like a wolf. Then the boat tips and you descend into the ravine, sliding sideways, down, down, down, and at the bottom the next steep wave crashes over your head. There is not only nothing equal to it, there is nothing second to it.

"Well!" shouts Big Shirley. "There goes the last of the sand!"

Hanta Yo! is astride the jutting point on the J-rig. She has a red bandanna tied around her neck and her hat pulled down to her eyebrows and has ridden the point like a bucking horse through the tall waves of Capsize Rapid and all the way down Mile Long, spurring the tubes so hard I'm surprised there is any air left in the boat. Her style is composed of (a) a death grip on the rigging and (b) her left arm held over her head.

In a calm stretch, Pam, the prettiest girl on the boat and a social worker with the homeless, asked Hanta Yo! to switch places before Big Drop 2.

"*I'm* riding the Big Drops!" shouts Hanta Yo!, yanking the rigging, rearing backwards, and kicking her heels into the tubes, three or four good whacks.

"This woman has found herself," Pam says to Robin. "And don't fuckin' get in her way"

By the time we reach Buttonhole rapid I have been sitting in the back beside Big Shirley so long that Hanta Yo!, a fellow Hoosier (how we regaled the girls with our school song!), takes pity on me and lets me have her place up on the jutting point. As we roar through Been Hurt, Hanta Yo! is yelling so many complicated instructions at me, telling me how to hold my mount, rear in rhythm, jab my spurs, and hold my left arm high in the air, that I crawl off the thing at the first opportunity and hand her the reins, she loves it so.

After eating half of an actual sandwich instead of a pound of peanut M&M's, Robin succumbs to heat exhaustion and dehydration during lunch break just before Big Drop 2. The sisters spring to action. Charnel brings cold wet clothes. Pam, Robin's best friend, pours water on her head. Sheri runs to get drinking water, and River, our medicine woman, squats in her black thong and places a red-mitted hand on the back of Robin's neck. When she reaches the third button, Robin, in the Great Baubo Seeing-Nipples spirit, half raises her head and says, "Watch out for my contact lenses."

Robin is propped, semiprostrate, with a big white sun hat tied over her face on the center tube in front of Big Shirley. Pam takes up a position on Robin's right, and as we turn into Big Drop 2—which is exactly equal to skidding into a high-speed crash, where if you're not anchored down, walls of water will wrap themselves around you and hustle you all the way down to Glen Canyon Dam—I look over and see that Pam is not hanging onto the ropes, but is holding down Robin. "Grab the rope. Pam!" I scream, and at that moment Hanta Yo! disappears on her bucking horse. Indeed, she is completely underwater, and all I can see is her left arm, bravely waving in the air.

Pam is a comely little thing who wears tiny pink camisoles and pastel-colored short-sets and washes her hair every day on the trip and has brought along a propane-powered hair curler. But by God, just like Sir Francis Bacon said, "If you have not a friend quit the stage," when we come through Big Drop 2, Robin is still on the boat, and it is Pam who kept her there.

At the party that night on the beach in Palmer Canyon we inhabit a higher sphere of thought. We grasp things in a true light. Our minds escape the prison of everyday speculations. In short, we are drunk as skunks. Catherine, in a see-through whirly Mexican skirt, looks like another person. "I'm so excited the death is over," she says. Hanta Yo! puts on lipstick. Robin appears fashionably late, dressed as Baubo's eyes—that is, she has stuck white tape eyelashes around her nipples, which glow in the dark, and she has drawn a nose on her belly button.

The next morning, our final day on the river, I have to return a camp mattress to Ann, the 911 dispatcher, and just for sheer exhilaration I walk across the beach stark naked, slathered in number 45. It is the tallest, tightest-thighed, highest-rumped, tit-bouncingest walk I've ever taken in my life, and the most lighthearted. The physical thrill is so great that when we arrive at crowded Hite Marina at Lake Powell, I strip off all my clothes again and, erect and contented, dive into the lake. Indeed, when you go new places, you get new ideas.

E. Jean Carroll is the author of Hunter: The Strange and Savage Life of Hunter S. Thompson *and the love-advice columnist for* Elle *magazine.*

Index of Contributors

Acknowledgments

Welcome to the "Who's Who" of Jen Leo. Are you looking for your name? For only $24.95 you can get your very own leather bound embossed and autographed copy.

Everyone on this page has already contributed much more than my weight in gold, and I thank the following old and new friends for their help with meals, shelter, and continued love and support before, during, and after this book project: The Bradys, the Lyons family, Donna & Dale Ball, the Wild Writing Women, the Heidrichs, the Villalon brothers, Seth & Leigh Presant, the Glezers, and the lads at BootsnAll.com.

Bags of platinum monkeys go to my self-appointed brothers and sisters who are consistently by my side no matter how my inane adventures turn up: Scott M. Gimple, Dan Buczaczer, Dana Welsh, and Heather Grennan.

When this book becomes a bestseller I will buy RTW tickets for the entire Travelers' Tales staff. Without their dedicated and careful hands, this book would be invisible. I owe many thanks to James O'Reilly for thinking I am funny and giving me this opportunity; heaps of thanks goes out to Larry Habegger and family for giving up his many late nights to ensure these stories were presentable; thanks also to Sean O'Reilly for his bottomless research files; Krista Holmstrom for her astute PR talent and friendship; and Chris Heidrich for his research contributions and daily comic relief. David Holmstrom gets a ticket too—without his creative insight this book would be topless. Our holiday will also include Raj Khadka, Wenda O'Reilly, Cynthia Lamb, Michele Weatherbee, Alex Brady, and Judy Johnson.

Susan Brady deserves a long, relaxing vacation for the unimaginable sweat, patience, and heart that went into coordinating this project from start to finish. Since I can't afford that, she'll just have to know that I recognize the overtime she put in for this book came from her love and personal investment in my life.

Last but not least, heartfelt appreciation to my dad Garry, Popo and Gung Gung, Jon, Val, Michelle, Katie, Lora, Jason, Barry, Tracey, and Josh Leo, Marylin Livingston, and the Idaho Livingstons—I can explore the world because I always have you to come home to.

"Women Who Run with No Clothes On" by E. Jean Carroll reprinted from the November 1993 issue of *Outside* magazine. Reprinted by permission from the author. Copyright © 1993.

Additional Credits (arranged alphabetically)

Selection from "Backpacking with a Belly in Indonesia" by Lara McKinley published with permission from the author. Copyright © 2003 by Lara McKinley.

Selection from "Bed in a Shed" by Dawn Bonker published with permission from the author. Copyright © 2003 by Dawn Bonker.

Selection from "Better Than Sex" by Carol Stigger published with permission from the author. Copyright © 2003 by Carol Stigger.

Selection from "Breasts" by Jennifer L. Leo published with permission from the author. Copyright © 2003 by Jennifer L. Leo.

Selection from "Cairo to Istanbul in a G-String" by Christine Michaud published with permission from the author. Copyright © 2003 by Christine Michaud.

Selection from "First Time in Asia" by Mary Noble published with permission from the author. Copyright © 2003 by Mary Noble.

Selection from "The Forbidden Throne" by Michelle Lott published with permission from the author. Copyright © 2003 by Michelle Lott.

Selections from *I'm Not Getting Older (I'm Getting Better At Denial)* by Leigh Anne Jasheway published by permission of the author. Copyright © 1999 by Leigh Anne Jasheway.

Selection from "The Importance of Packing" by Joan Churchill published with permission from the author. Copyright © 2003 by Joan Churchill.

Selection from "In Quest of Plus Value" by Heather Bloch published with permission from the author. Copyright © 2003 by Heather Bloch.

Selection from "Italian Lessons" by Jacqueline Harmon Butler published with permission from the author. Copyright © 2003 by Jacqueline Harmon Butler.

Selection from "Joshua Tree" by Rachel Quinn published with permission from the author. Copyright © 2003 by Rachel Quinn.

Selection from "The Joys of Travel" by Susan Brady published with permission from the author. Copyright © 2003 by Susan Brady.

Selection from "La Doccia Vita" by Kelly Simon published with permission from the author. Copyright © 2003 by Kelly Simon.

Selection from "My Handbag, My Self" by Robin Epstein published with permission from the author. Copyright © 2003 by Robin Epstein.

Selection from "On the Way to Shameless" by Loren Drummond published with permission from the author. Copyright © 2003 by Loren Drummond.

Selection from "Pack Light" by Anita Kugelstadt published with permission from the author. Copyright © 2003 by Anita Kugelstadt.

Selection from *Shitting Pretty: How to Stay Clean and Healthy While Traveling* by Dr. Jane Wilson-Howarth reprinted by permission of Travelers' Tales, Inc. Copyright © 2000 by Jane Wilson-Howarth.

Selection from "A Taste of the Night" by Susan Brady published with permission from the author. Copyright © 2003 by Susan Brady.

Selection from *Why I'm Like This: True Stories* by Cynthia Kaplan reprinted by permission of HarperCollins Publishers, Inc. Copyright © 2002 by Cynthia Kaplan.

About the Editor

Jennifer L. Leo is a Chinese-American born with a gift for gab and a hunger for an everlasting craps game. She lives to love—love ice cream, fish tacos, movies, Australia, and men. She is co-editor of *A Woman's Path*, and her writing has also appeared in *Wild Writing Women: Stories of World Travel, A Woman's Passion for Travel, The Adventure of Food,* Lonely Planet World Food Guides *Hong Kong* and *California*, BootsNAll.com, and other books in the Travelers' Tales series. When not working on a career in print and online travel publishing, Jen fantasizes about her dream job of being a jewelry thief and stay-at-home mom. For practice she lifts brown mustard from burger joints and borrows children from her friends. Her nomadic bloodline can be traced back five generations to Canton, China. Between wanderings, Jen encourages others to follow their travel writing passions on her web site, WrittenRoad.com. Keep up with her adventures on www.JenLeo.com.

Travelers' Tales Classics

COAST TO COAST
A Journey Across 1950s America
By Jan Morris
ISBN 1-885-211-79-1
$16.95

After reporting on the first Everest ascent in 1953, Morris spent a year journeying by car, train, ship, and aircraft across the United States. In her brilliant prose, Morris records with exuberance and curiosity a time of innocence in the U.S.

THE ROYAL ROAD TO ROMANCE
By Richard Halliburton
ISBN 1-885-211-53-8
$14.95

"Laughing at hardships, dreaming of beauty, ardent for adventure, Halliburton has managed to sing into the pages of this glorious book his own exultant spirit of youth and freedom."
—*Chicago Post*

THE RIVERS RAN EAST
By Leonard Clark
ISBN 1-885-211-66-X
$16.95

Clark is the original Indiana Jones, relaying a breathtaking account of his search for the legendary El Dorado gold in the Amazon.

THERE'S NO TOILET PAPER...ON THE ROAD LESS TRAVELED
The Best of Travel Humor and Misadventure
Edited by Doug Lansky
ISBN 1-885-211-27-9
$12.95

Humor Book of the Year —Independent Publisher's Book Award

ForeWord Gold Medal Winner—Humor Book of the Year

TRADER HORN
A Young Man's Astounding Adventures in 19th Century Equatorial Africa
By Alfred Aloysius Horn
ISBN 1-885-211-81-3
$16.95

Here is the stuff of legends—tale of thrills and danger, wild beasts, serpents, and savages. An unforgettable and vivid portrait of a vanished late-19th century Africa.

UNBEATEN TRACKS IN JAPAN
By Isabella L. Bird
ISBN 1-885-211-57-0
$14.95

Isabella Bird was one of the most adventurous women travelers of the 19th century with journeys to Tibet, Canada, Korea, Turkey, Hawaii, and Japan. A fascinating read for anyone interested in women's travel, spirituality, and Asian culture.

Travel Humor

NOT SO FUNNY WHEN IT HAPPENED
The Best of Travel Humor and Misadventure
Edited by Tim Cahill
ISBN 1-885-211-55-4
$12.95

Laugh with Bill Bryson, Dave Barry, Anne Lamott, Adair Lara, and many more.

LAST TROUT IN VENICE
The Far-Flung Escapades of an Accidental Adventurer
By Doug Lansky
ISBN 1-885-211-63-5
$14.95

"Traveling with Doug Lansky might result in a considerably shortened life expectancy...but what a way to go."
—Tony Wheeler, Lonely Planet Publications

Women's Travel

A WOMAN'S PASSION FOR TRAVEL
More True Stories from A Woman's World
Edited by Marybeth Bond & Pamela Michael
ISBN 1-885-211-36-8
$17.95

"A diverse and gripping series of stories!" —Arlene Blum, author of *Annapurna: A Woman's Place*

A WOMAN'S WORLD
True Stories of Life on the Road
Edited by Marybeth Bond
Introduction by Dervla Murphy
ISBN 1-885-211-06-6
$17.95

—★★★—

Winner of the Lowell Thomas Award for Best Travel Book—Society of American Travel Writers

WOMEN IN THE WILD
True Stories of Adventure and Connection
Edited by Lucy McCauley
ISBN 1-885-211-21-X
$17.95

"A spiritual, moving, and totally female book to take you around the world and back." —*Mademoiselle*

A MOTHER'S WORLD
Journeys of the Heart
Edited by Marybeth Bond & Pamela Michael
ISBN 1-885-211-26-0
$14.95

"These stories remind us that motherhood is one of the great unifying forces in the world" —*San Francisco Examiner*

Food

ADVENTURES IN WINE
True Stories of Vineyards and Vintages around the World
Edited by Thom Elkjer
ISBN 1-885-211-80-5
$17.95

Humanity, community, and brotherhood comprise the marvelous virtues of the wine world. This collection toasts the warmth and wonders of this large, extended family in stories by travelers who are wine novices and experts alike.

FOOD (Updated)
A Taste of the Road
Edited by Richard Sterling
Introduction by Margo True
ISBN 1-885-211-77-5
$18.95

Silver Medal Winner of the Lowell Thomas Award for Best Travel Book—Society of American Travel Writers

HER FORK IN THE ROAD
Women Celebrate Food and Travel
Edited by Lisa Bach
ISBN 1-885-211-71-6
$16.95

A savory sampling of stories by some of the best writers in and out of the food and travel fields.

THE ADVENTURE OF FOOD
True Stories of Eating Everything
Edited by Richard Sterling
ISBN 1-885-211-37-6
$17.95

"These stories are bound to whet appetites for more than food." —*Publishers Weekly*

Spiritual Travel

THE SPIRITUAL GIFTS OF TRAVEL
The Best of Travelers' Tales
Edited by James O'Reilly and Sean O'Reilly
ISBN 1-885-211-69-4
$16.95

A collection of favorite stories of transformation on the road from our award-winning Travelers' Tales series that shows the myriad ways travel indelibly alters our inner landscapes.

THE WAY OF THE WANDERER
Discover Your True Self Through Travel
By David Yeadon
ISBN 1-885-211-60-0
$14.95

Experience transformation through travel with this delightful, illustrated collection by award-winning author David Yeadon.

PILGRIMAGE
Adventures of the Spirit
Edited by Sean O'Reilly & James O'Reilly
Introduction by Phil Cousineau
ISBN 1-885-211-56-2
$16.95

★★★

ForeWord Silver Medal Winner — Travel Book of the Year

A WOMAN'S PATH
Women's Best Spiritual Travel Writing
Edited by Lucy McCauley, Amy G. Carlson & Jennifer Leo
ISBN 1-885-211-48-1
$16.95

"A sensitive exploration of women's lives that have been unexpectedly and spiritually touched by travel experiences.... Highly recommended."
—*Library Journal*

THE ROAD WITHIN
True Stories of Transformation and the Soul
Edited by Sean O'Reilly, James O'Reilly & Tim O'Reilly
ISBN 1-885-211-19-8
$17.95

★★★

Best Spiritual Book—Independent Publisher's Book Award

THE ULTIMATE JOURNEY
Inspiring Stories of Living and Dying
James O'Reilly, Sean O'Reilly & Richard Sterling
ISBN 1-885-211-38-4
$17.95

"A glorious collection of writings about the ultimate adventure. A book to keep by one's bedside—and close to one's heart." —Philip Zaleski, editor, *The Best Spiritual Writing series*

Adventure

TESTOSTERONE PLANET
True Stories from a Man's World
Edited by Sean O'Reilly, Larry Habegger & James O'Reilly
ISBN 1-885-211-43-0
$17.95

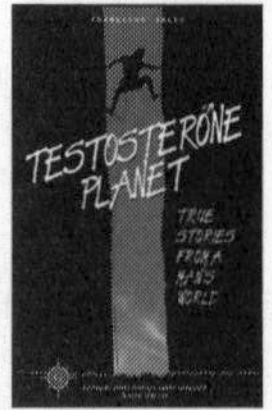

Thrills and laughter with some of today's best writers: Sebastian Junger, Tim Cahill, Bill Bryson, and Jon Krakauer.

DANGER!
True Stories of Trouble and Survival
Edited by James O'Reilly, Larry Habegger & Sean O'Reilly
ISBN 1-885-211-32-5
$17.95

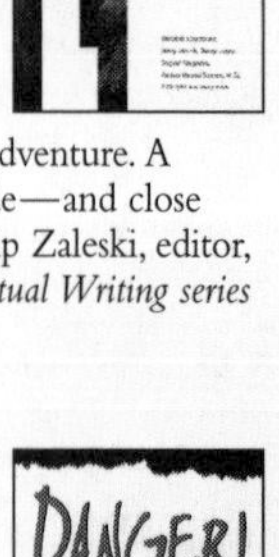

"Exciting...for those who enjoy living on the edge or prefer to read the survival stories of others, this is a good pick."
—*Library Journal*

Special Interest

365 TRAVEL
A Daily Book of Journeys, Meditations, and Adventures
Edited by Lisa Bach
ISBN 1-885-211-67-8
$14.95
An illuminating collection of travel wisdom and adventures that reminds us all of the lessons we learn while on the road.

FAMILY TRAVEL
The Farther You Go, the Closer You Get
Edited by Laura Manske
ISBN 1-885-211-33-3
$17.95
"This is family travel at its finest." —*Working Mother*

THE GIFT OF BIRDS
True Encounters with Avian Spirits
Edited by Larry Habegger & Amy G. Carlson
ISBN 1-885-211-41-4
$17.95
"These are all wonderful, entertaining stories offering a *bird's-eye view!* of our avian friends."
—*Booklist*

THE GIFT OF RIVERS
True Stories of Life on the Water
Edited by Pamela Michael
Introduction by Robert Hass
ISBN 1-885-211-42-2
$14.95
"*The Gift of Rivers* is a soulful compendium of wonderful stories that illuminate, educate, inspire, and delight."
—David Brower, Chairman of Earth Island Institute

LOVE & ROMANCE
True Stories of Passion on the Road
Edited by Judith Babcock Wylie
ISBN 1-885-211-18-X
$17.95
"A wonderful book to read by a crackling fire."
—*Romantic Traveling*

A DOG'S WORLD
True Stories of Man's Best Friend on the Road
Edited by Christine Hunsicker
ISBN 1-885-211-23-6
$12.95
This extraordinary collection includes stories by John Steinbeck, Helen Thayer, James Herriot, Pico Iyer, and many others.

THE GIFT OF TRAVEL
The Best of Travelers' Tales
Edited by Larry Habegger, James O'Reilly & Sean O'Reilly
ISBN 1-885-211-25-2
$14.95
"Like gourmet chefs in a French market, the editors of Travelers' Tales pick, sift, and prod their way through the weighty shelves of contemporary travel writing, creaming off the very best."
—William Dalrymple, author of *City of Djinns*

Travel Advice

SHITTING PRETTY
How to Stay Clean and Healthy While Traveling
By Dr. Jane Wilson-Howarth
ISBN 1-885-211-47-3
$12.95
A light-hearted book about a serious subject for millions of travelers—staying healthy on the road—written by international health expert, Dr. Jane Wilson-Howarth.

THE FEARLESS SHOPPER
How to Get the Best Deals on the Planet
By Kathy Borrus
ISBN 1-885-211-39-2
$14.95
"Anyone who reads *The Fearless Shopper* will come away a smarter, more responsible shopper and a more curious, culturally attuned traveler."
—Jo Mancuso, *The Shopologist*

GUTSY WOMEN
More Travel Tips and Wisdom for the Road
By Marybeth Bond
ISBN 1-885-211-61-9
$12.95
Second Edition—Packed with funny, instructive, and inspiring advice for women heading out to see the world.

SAFETY AND SECURITY FOR WOMEN WHO TRAVEL
By Sheila Swan & Peter Laufer
ISBN 1-885-211-29-5
$12.95
A must for every woman traveler!

THE FEARLESS DINER
Travel Tips and Wisdom for Eating around the World
By Richard Sterling
ISBN 1-885-211-22-8
$7.95
Combines practical advice on foodstuffs, habits, and etiquette, with hilarious accounts of others' eating adventures.

THE PENNY PINCHER'S PASSPORT TO LUXURY TRAVEL
The Art of Cultivating Preferred Customer Status
By Joel L. Widzer
ISBN 1-885-211-31-7
$12.95
Proven techniques on how to travel first class at discount prices, even if you're not a frequent flyer.

GUTSY MAMAS
Travel Tips and Wisdom for Mothers on the Road
By Marybeth Bond
ISBN 1-885-211-20-1
$7.95
A delightful guide for mothers traveling with their children—or without them!

Destination Titles:
True Stories of Life on the Road

AMERICA
Edited by Fred Setterberg
ISBN 1-885-211-28-7
$19.95

AMERICAN SOUTHWEST
Edited by Sean O'Reilly & James O'Reilly
ISBN 1-885-211-58-9
$17.95

AUSTRALIA
Edited by Larry Habegger
ISBN 1-885-211-40-6
$17.95

BRAZIL
Edited by Annette Haddad & Scott Doggett
Introduction by Alex Shoumatoff
ISBN 1-885-211-11-2
$17.95

CENTRAL AMERICA
Edited by Larry Habegger & Natanya Pearlman
ISBN 1-885-211-74-0
$17.95

CUBA
Edited by Tom Miller
ISBN 1-885-211-62-7
$17.95

FRANCE (**Updated**)
Edited by James O'Reilly, Larry Habegger & Sean O'Reilly
ISBN 1-885-211-73-2
$18.95

GRAND CANYON
Edited by Sean O'Reilly, James O'Reilly & Larry Habegger
ISBN 1-885-211-34-1
$17.95

GREECE
Edited by Larry Habegger, Sean O'Reilly & Brian Alexander
ISBN 1-885-211-52-X
$17.95

HAWAI'I
Edited by Rick & Marcie Carroll
ISBN 1-885-211-35-X
$17.95

HONG KONG
Edited by James O'Reilly, Larry Habegger & Sean O'Reilly
ISBN 1-885-211-03-1
$17.95

INDIA
Edited by James O'Reilly & Larry Habegger
ISBN 1-885-211-01-5
$17.95

IRELAND
Edited by James O'Reilly, Larry Habegger & Sean O'Reilly
ISBN 1-885-211-46-5
$17.95

ITALY (Updated)
Edited by Anne Calcagno
Introduction by Jan Morris
ISBN 1-885-211-72-4
$18.95

JAPAN
Edited by Donald W. George & Amy G. Carlson
ISBN 1-885-211-04-X
$17.95

MEXICO (Updated)
Edited by James O'Reilly & Larry Habegger
ISBN 1-885-211-59-7
$17.95

NEPAL
Edited by Rajendra S. Khadka
ISBN 1-885-211-14-7
$17.95

PARIS
Edited by James O'Reilly, Larry Habegger & Sean O'Reilly
ISBN 1-885-211-10-4
$17.95

SAN FRANCISCO
Edited by James O'Reilly, Larry Habegger & Sean O'Reilly
ISBN 1-885-211-08-2
$17.95

SPAIN (Updated)
Edited by Lucy McCauley
ISBN 1-885-211-78-3
$19.95

THAILAND (Updated)
Edited by James O'Reilly & Larry Habegger
ISBN 1-885-211-75-9
$18.95

TIBET
Edited by James O'Reilly, Larry Habegger, & Kim Morris
ISBN 1-885-211-76-7
$18.95

TUSCANY
Edited by James O'Reilly, & Tara Austen Weaver
ISBN 1-885-211-68-6
$16.95